Let's Microwave!

EXCITING SEASONAL RECIPES AND BUSY-DAY HINTS

BY
CARALAN DAMS B.Sc., Home Economics

Front Cover
Western Tourtière, page 116

Let's Microwave!
by:
Caralan Dams, B.Sc., Home Economics

Second Printing — October, 1987

Copyright © 1987 by
Delta Publishing Ltd.
P.O. Box 5411 Station "A"
Calgary, Alberta, Canada   T2H 1X8

Canadian Cataloguing in Publication Data

Dams, Caralan, 1956-
  Let's microwave!

Includes index.
ISBN 0-919845-51-7

1. Microwave cookery.   2. Holiday cookery.
I. Title.
TX832.D34 1987   641.5'882   C87-098062-9

Photography by:
Ross C. (Hutch) Hutchinson
Bolli & Hutchinson Photographic Design Ltd.
Calgary, Alberta

Dishes and Accessories Compliments of:
Brandi's Kitchen Boutique Ltd., Calgary
Corning Canada Inc. generously donated
    Corning Ware cookware
Happy Cooker Emporium, Calgary
Flowers by Oak Bay Florist Ltd., Calgary

Designed, Printed and Produced in Canada by
Centax of Canada
Publishing Consultant and Food Stylist — Margo Embury
Design by Blair Fraser
1048 Fleury Street
Regina, Saskatchewan, Canada   S4N 4W8
(306) 359-3737
Toll-Free 1-800-667-5844

TABLE OF CONTENTS

The recipes in this cookbook have been tested on a 700 watt output oven. Your timings may vary slightly. Whenever possible, use the descriptions given in the recipes as a final indicator.

THIS BOOK IS DEDICATED WITH LOVE AND THANKS TO MY MOM AND DAD

WITH THANKS TO:

Margo Embury of Centax of Canada for her patience, sense of humor and expertise in all phases and stages of the production of this cookbook. Margo excels in her profession, and is an invaluable asset to the Canadian cookbook industry.

Kathy Grandia for her help during the food photography. Kathy's creative flair and sense of humour were much appreciated.

Iveah Hutchison for her help, advice and support since the onset of writing Let's Microwave!

Janice Krakowski, another Calgary microwave instructor, and personal friend for sharing her microwave tips and hints with me.

Marlene McCullough, Roger Glover and all the staff at C.I.B.C. for being so easy to work with.

Svea and Bob Murray, my Mom and Dad, for sharing their recipes and new and different food experiences with me. Mom and Dad are always there to help when the going gets a little bumpy.

My many friends and family who were kind enough to share recipes with me.

A very special thanks to my husband Bob, for sharing and caring at all times during the writing of this book. Besides being a professional Forester/Agrologist, husband and father, Bob has also taken on roles of editor, computer expert, food tester, business advisor, secretary, and psychologist.

NEW YEAR'S DAY

New Year's Day is a great time for family parties and reunions and a time for New Year Resolutions - many of which are not kept very long! Cheer in the the New Year with an array of exciting dishes - a wealth of appetizers, and a tasty meal - straying somewhat from the traditional turkey feast. Whether you celebrate it as the finale of the old or the kickoff for the new, New Year's is the perfect time to entertain friends and family alike. Do as much as you can in advance, relax with the help of your microwave and ring in the new!

APPETIZER SALMON PÂTÉ

This tasty pâté can be molded and served with crackers and party bread slices, or it can be spooned into cherry tomato halves, prior to geling, and set right in the cherry tomatoes.

2 tbsp.	unflavored gelatin (2 envelopes)	30 mL
¾ cup	cold water	175 mL
1 cup	salad dressing or mayonnaise	250 mL
15 oz.	canned salmon, drained, flaked	439 g
½ cup	finely chopped celery	125 mL
¼ cup	finely chopped green pepper	50 mL
1 tsp.	finely chopped onion	5 mL
1 tsp.	dried dill weed	5 mL
½ tsp.	Beau Monde Seasoning	2 mL
1 tsp.	lemon juice	5 mL
¾ cup	whipping cream, whipped	175 mL

1. Place gelatin and cold water in a small bowl. Microwave on **HIGH** for 1 - 2 minutes until gelatin is dissolved.

2. Add salad dressing or mayonnaise, mixing until blended. Refrigerate until the mixture is just starting to set.

3. Stir in remaining ingredients, folding in the whipped cream last.

4. Pour into a lightly oiled 4-cup (1 L) mold, or spoon into approximately 30 hollowed cherry tomato halves. Chill until firm.

5. Loosen mold by submerging in hot water for 10 - 15 seconds. Invert onto a bed of leaf lettuce.

Serves 10 - 12.

See photograph page 112A.

CHEESE BALL

This delicious cheese ball is an excellent appetizer to take to a party, because it packs well (i.e. it won't spill all over your car!) and requires no last-minute preparation.

¼ cup	finely chopped green pepper	50 mL
¼ cup	finely chopped green onion	50 mL
1 tsp.	butter or margarine	5 mL
14 oz.	package cream cheese	400 g
2 cups	shredded Cheddar cheese	500 mL
4 oz.	blue cheese, crumbled	125 g
1 tbsp.	chopped pimiento	15 mL
2 tsp.	prepared horseradish	10 mL
2 tsp.	Worcestershire sauce	10 mL
1	clove garlic, minced	1
½ cup	chopped pecans	125 mL

1. Combine green pepper, onion and butter in a small bowl. Microwave on **HIGH** for 30 - 45 seconds, or until the vegetables are tender-crisp, stirring once.

2. Place cream cheese in a large bowl. Microwave on **MEDIUM** for 1 - 1½ minutes or until softened. Stir in remaining ingredients except pecans. Shape into a ball.

3. Wrap in plastic wrap. Chill 2 - 3 hours. Unwrap; roll in pecans. Serve with assorted crackers.

Serves 10 - 12. Recipe may be halved.

See photograph page 112A.

CHEDDAR JALAPEÑO FONDUE

It seems that any selection of appetizers just isn't complete without including some trendy Mexican Cuisine. This particular fondue is tasty served with raw vegetables, tortilla chips or crusty bread.

½ lb.	Cheddar cheese	250 g
½ lb.	Gruyère or Swiss cheese	250 g
1 cup	dry white wine	250 mL
2 tsp.	water	10 mL
2 tsp.	cornstarch	10 mL
2 tbsp.	finely chopped jalapeño peppers	30 mL
2 tsp.	finely minced garlic	10 mL
½ tsp.	dried coriander	2 mL

CHEDDAR JALAPEÑO FONDUE (cont'd.)

1. Grate cheeses, and place in a medium-sized bowl. Add wine. Microwave on **HIGH** for 3 - 6 minutes or until the cheeses are completely melted and the mixture is smooth.

2. Blend the water and the cornstarch. Add remaining ingredients. Stir into the cheese mixture. Microwave on **HIGH** for an additional 2 - 3 minutes or until the mixture thickens.

3. Keep warm over a small flame or on a warming plate. Do not allow the fondue to cool, as it thickens rapidly.

Serves 10.

See photograph page 112A.

SHRIMP WRAP-UPS

A tasty appetizer made similarly to Rumaki, except with the ever popular shrimp as a filler.

8	slices of bacon	8
8	uncooked large shrimp, peeled, deveined	8
1	green pepper, cut into 16 pieces	1
2 tbsp.	soy sauce	30 mL
2 tbsp.	white wine or water	30 mL
2 tbsp.	chili sauce	30 mL
2 tbsp.	plum or grape jelly	30 mL

1. Arrange 4 slices of bacon in the bottom of a square casserole or on a roasting rack. Arrange the remaining 4 slices on top of, and perpendicular to, the bottom 4. You should now have a latticework of bacon in the bottom of the casserole dish.

2. Cover and microwave on **HIGH** for 4 - 5 minutes until the bacon is slightly brown but not fully cooked or crisp.

3. Cut the shrimp in half lengthwise. Cut bacon slices in half. Wrap a piece of shrimp and green pepper in each bacon piece. Secure with a toothpick. Place in a 9 x 9-inch (22 cm) glass baking dish.

4. Mix remaining ingredients, in a small bowl. Pour over the wrap-ups.

5. Cover and refrigerate, no longer than 8 hours, stirring once or twice. To serve, microwave on **HIGH** for 3 - 4 minutes or until the shrimp is opaque, and the bacon crisp.

Makes 16 appetizers.

See photograph page 112A.

RUMAKI CANAPES

An unusual slant on a popular appetizer, this tasty rendition is by Jean Waterworth, a Micro-Cooking Centre consultant.

½ cup	water	125 mL
1 tsp.	chicken bouillon powder	5 mL
½ lb.	chicken livers	250 g
6	strips bacon	6
1 tbsp.	soy sauce	15 mL
½ tsp.	onion powder	2 mL
½ tsp.	dry mustard	2 mL
¼ tsp.	nutmeg	1 mL
¼ cup	dry sherry	50 mL
dash	Tabasco sauce	dash
7¾ oz.	drained, chopped water chestnuts	220 g

1. Combine water, chicken bouillon and livers in a 1-quart (1 L) casserole. Cover and microwave on **HIGH** for 4 - 5 minutes, stirring once, or until the chicken livers are no longer pink. Drain.

2. Place bacon on a roasting rack or in the bottom of a small casserole.

3. Cover and microwave on **HIGH** for 4 - 5 minutes or until crisply cooked. Crumble and set aside.

4. Put livers, soy sauce, onion and mustard powders, nutmeg and sherry into a blender or food processor. Blend until smooth. Add Tabasco sauce sparingly. Stir in the water chestnuts and bacon.

5. Spread thickly on toast triangles, or crackers. Microwave on **MEDIUM HIGH** 1 - 2 minutes per 12 canapes. Garnish with a slice of olive or pimiento if desired.

Makes 24 canapes.

For a quick appetizer, drain a 7¾ oz. (284 mL) can of artichoke hearts. Arrange on a glass plate and top with ⅓ cup (75 mL) dry, seasoned bread crumbs, ¼ cup (50 mL) grated Parmesan cheese and 4 tbsp. (60 mL) of Italian dressing. Microwave on HIGH for 3 - 4 minutes.

To microwave clams in the shell, place 6 in a circular pattern on a glass pie plate. Cover with wet paper towel and microwave on HIGH for 3 - 4 minutes, or until the clams open.

SWEET AND SOUR TURKEY BITES

Ground turkey is a delicious change from ground beef, and very appropriate at this time of year.

TURKEY BITES:

2 lbs.	ground raw turkey meat	1	kg
2	eggs, beaten	2	
1 cup	dry bread crumbs	250	mL
1 tsp.	salt	5	mL
½ tsp.	pepper	2	mL
2 tbsp.	butter or margarine, melted	30	mL

SWEET AND SOUR SAUCE:

1 cup	pineapple juice	250	mL
1 cup	chicken broth	250	mL
½ cup	white granulated sugar	125	mL
⅓ cup	red wine vinegar	75	mL
2 tbsp.	soy sauce	45	mL
2 tbsp.	cornstarch	45	mL

1. Mix turkey, eggs, bread crumbs, salt, pepper and butter together lightly. Shape into small uniform balls. Place half of the bites on a large circular platter.

2. Microwave on **HIGH** for 6 - 7 minutes or until the bites are no longer pink. Repeat with remaining half. Set aside.

3. Combine sauce ingredients in a large bowl. Stir well to dissolve sugar and cornstarch.

4. Microwave on **HIGH** for 2 - 4 minutes, stirring every 1 minute, until the sauce comes to a boil and becomes clear. Boil on **HIGH** for 1 complete minute.

5. Add the turkey bites to the sauce and microwave on **MEDIUM** for 4 - 6 minutes, stirring after 3 minutes.

Makes 70 appetizers. If you can't find preground turkey meat, buy a 2 lb. (1 kg) turkey breast and put it through a meat grinder or a food processor.

If freezing ground beef, divide into desired amounts. Shape into a cylinder-like shape and then make a depression in the center with a wooden spoon. This makes for much easier and more even defrosting.

ESCARGOT-STUFFED MUSHROOMS

Treat yourself! Serve with lots of bread for dipping the butter.

24	large mushrooms, stems removed	24
24	Escargot	24

BUTTER:

½ cup	butter	125 mL
2	cloves garlic, crushed	2
2 tbsp.	parsley	30 mL
¼ tsp.	lemon juice	1 mL
1 tsp.	Creole seasoning	5 mL

1. Arrange the mushrooms, cap side down, in a casserole.

2. Cream butter and add garlic, parsley, lemon juice and seasoning. Put ¼ tsp. (1 mL) of the garlic butter into each cap. Top with 1 escargot.

3. Cover with another ¼ tsp. (1 mL) of garlic butter. Refrigerate filled caps several hours or overnight.

4. Microwave on **MEDIUM** for 5 - 6 minutes, covered loosely with waxed paper. Escargot may pop. Microwave until butter bubbles.

Serves 6. May be halved.

GREEN BEANS CAESAR

Green beans take well to herb flavors. What better way to start off the new year than with a different twist on an all-time favorite.

4 cups	fresh green beans	1 L
	OR	
20 oz.	frozen green beans	600 g
¼ cup	butter or margarine	50 mL
¾ cup	minced green onion	175 mL
¼ cup	minced celery	50 mL
1 clove	garlic, minced or pressed	1
¼ cup	minced parsley	50 mL
¼ tsp.	dried rosemary	1 mL
¼ tsp.	dried basil leaves	1 mL
¾ tsp.	salt	4 mL
1 tsp.	lemon juice	5 mL
1 tsp.	Worcestershire sauce	5 mL
	Parmesan bread croutons	

1. Trim fresh green beans. Cut into diagonal 1-inch (2.2 cm) pieces. Place in a small bowl. Add ¼ cup (50 mL) water, cover, and microwave on **HIGH** for 7 - 9 minutes, or until tender. If using frozen green beans, microwave in exactly the same manner. Drain. Cool Completely.

GREEN BEANS CAESAR (cont'd.)

2. Microwave butter, onion, celery and garlic in a small bowl on **HIGH** for 2 - 3 minutes or until the vegetables are tender. Add seasonings. Microwave on **LOW** for an additional 10 minutes. Cool completely.

3. Transfer drained beans to serving platter. Fold in onion and celery mixture, tossing to blend. Top with the croutons. Serve immediately.

Serves 4. For 2 servings halve the ingredients, for 8 servings double.

SCALLOPS ITALIENNE

By New Year's Day most of us are craving for something other than turkey and ham. Treat your tastebuds to tender, delicious scallops.

1½	lb.	frozen or fresh scallops	750 g
1	cup	dry white wine or water	250 mL
1	cup	water	250 mL
2		bay leaves	2
6		black peppercorns	6
1	tsp.	salt	5 mL
½	lb.	fresh mushrooms, quartered	250 g
4	tbsp.	butter or margarine	60 mL
1	cup	whipping cream	250 mL
1		egg, slightly beaten	1
8	oz.	uncooked egg noodles	250 g
¾	cup	grated Parmesan cheese	175 mL

1. Thaw scallops if frozen. Cut any large scallops in half.

2. Microwave wine, water, bay leaves, peppercorns and salt in a large bowl, on **HIGH** for 3 - 4 minutes or until it just begins to boil.

3. Add scallops. Microwave for an additional 2 - 3 minutes on **HIGH** until the scallops are white. Remove scallops. Continuing microwaving the liquid on **HIGH** until reduced to ½ cup (125 mL).

4. Microwave mushrooms and 2 tbsp. (30 mL) butter on **HIGH** for 3 - 4 minutes, until mushrooms are tender and transparent. Remove bay leaves from liquid. Add ¾ cup (175 mL) cream, scallops, and mushrooms to reduced liquid. Microwave on **HIGH** for 1 minute. Mix a little hot liquid into beaten egg. Add whole egg back to hot liquid. Stir well. Microwave on **HIGH** for 1 - 2 minutes or until thickened slightly.

5. Cook noodles conventionally until firm but tender. Melt remaining butter on **HIGH** for 30 seconds. Add noodles, tossing until hot. Add remaining cream. Quickly stir in ½ of the Parmesan Cheese.

6. Turn noodles into hot serving platter. Top with scallop and mushroom mixture. Sprinkle with remaining cheese. Serve immediately.

Serves 4.

CHOCOLATE ALMOND CHEESECAKE

A delicious cheesecake, loaded with great taste and yes, calories too!

CRUST:

1½ cups	chocolate-wafer crumbs	375 g
1 cup	blanched almonds, lightly toasted and finely chopped	250 mL
¼ cup	granulated white sugar	50 mL
⅓ cup	butter or margarine, softened	75 mL

FILLING:

24 oz.	room-temperature cream cheese	750 g
1 cup	white granulated sugar	250 mL
4	eggs	4
⅓ cup	heavy cream	75 mL
¼ cup	almond-flavored liqueur	50 mL
1 tsp.	vanilla	5 mL

TOPPING:

2 cups	sour cream	500 mL
1 tbsp.	white granulated sugar	15 mL
1 tsp.	vanilla	5 mL
	toasted slivered almonds	

1. Combine crumbs, almonds, sugar and softened butter. Press very gently into the bottom and sides of a 10-inch (24 cm) circular ovenproof glass dish. Microwave on **HIGH** for 2 minutes. Cool.

2. Beat cream cheese and sugar until combined. Beat in eggs one at a time, beating well after each addition. Beat in cream, almond-flavored liqueur and vanilla, beating until mixture is light and smooth.

3. Pour batter into the cooled chocolate shell and microwave, covered, on **MEDIUM HIGH** for 12 minutes. Let stand for 5 minutes. Cake will not be set.

4. Prepare topping by combining the sour cream, sugar and vanilla in a mixing bowl. Spread evenly over the top of cake. Microwave on **MEDIUM HIGH** for an additional 2 - 3 minutes. Cake should be set. Remove from the microwave and let cool completely.

5. Loosely cover cake with a sheet of foil or plastic wrap and refrigerate overnight. It is important to refrigerate cake overnight before serving. Press slivered almonds around the top edge for decoration before serving.

Serves 8 - 10. Recipe may be halved by halving all ingredients and cooking times. Use an 8-inch (20 cm) cake pan.

VALENTINE'S DAY

The Feast of St. Valentine is a Christian festival originating in A.D. 496. This has little if anything to do with the custom observed by people in many countries, of sending cards, flowers or presents to one's sweetheart. Most of us prefer to think of this day as a day for love, romance and sentimental times. Surprise your sweetheart with a box-full of chocolate treats to create a memory that will be cherished forever. Prepare a delicious menu for two. To add elegance to your Valentine dinner, place a rose on each napkin. For extra fun, hide Valentine cards where they will be discovered throughout the day... inside a coat pocket, a lunch box or even in the refrigerator.

SPINACH SALAD WITH POPPY SEED DRESSING

This terrific salad is superb with almost every meal.

½ head	spinach, torn into bite-size pieces	½	
1	green onion, chopped	1	
½ cup	mandarin orange segments, drained, or any seasonal fruit	125	mL
7	grapes, washed and halved	7	
½ cup	white granulated sugar	125	mL
1 tsp.	salt	5	mL
1 tsp.	dry mustard	5	mL
⅓ cup	white vinegar	75	mL
1 tbsp.	lemon juice	15	mL
1 cup	salad oil	250	mL
1½ tbsp.	poppy seeds	20	mL

1. Toss spinach, onion, oranges and grapes in a large bowl.

2. Combine sugar, salt, mustard, vinegar and lemon juice in a small bowl. Add oil and poppy seeds, Whisk well. Microwave on **HIGH** for 30 seconds to 1 minute or until slightly warm. Cool completely.

3. Pour ½ of dressing over salad and serve immediately.

Serves 2. For 4, double salad ingredients. Don't double dressing.

NOTE: Refrigerate leftover dressing, use within 2 weeks.

See photograph page 48A.

STUFFED CORNISH HENS WITH ORANGE SAUCE

This recipe can be doubled if you wish to share your Valentine with others or you can light the candles, put on some soft music, and enjoy this tasty treat, just the 2 of you.

2½ cups	very hot tap water	625 mL
¼ cup	frozen orange juice concentrate	50 mL
6 oz.	pkg. long-grain and wild rice	170 g
4	slices bacon, cooked, crumbled	4
2	Cornish hens, 1 lb. (500 g) each	2
⅓ cup	honey	75 mL
¼ cup	frozen orange juice concentrate	50 mL
¼ cup	orange marmalade	50 mL
1 tbsp.	orange brandy liqueur (optional)	15 mL
½ tsp.	soy sauce	2 mL

1. Combine water, first amount of orange juice concentrate, and rice in a 2-quart (2L) casserole. Cover and microwave on **MEDIUM** for 25 - 30 minutes or until rice is tender. Stir in crumbled bacon.

2. Stuff hens with rice mixture, taking care not to stuff too firmly. There will be some rice remaining. Reserve for other uses. With a cotton string, tie legs together. Place on a roasting rack OR elevate on inverted saucers in a pie dish. Cover with waxed paper and microwave on **MEDIUM HIGH** for 10 minutes.

3. Meanwhile, mix together remaining ingredients. Baste hens that have been partially microwaved with the orange mixture. Return basted hens to microwave and continue microwaving on **MEDIUM HIGH** for 5 - 8 minutes or until the juice runs clear from the hens and there is no longer any pink next to the bones. Let stand, 10 minutes, before serving.

Serves 2. For 4, double the sauce ingredients and use 4 Cornish hens. Do not double the rice mixture as there is already enough to stuff 4 hens. Microwave the hens for 20 minutes on MEDIUM HIGH. Baste and continue microwaving on MEDIUM HIGH for an additional 8 - 12 minutes.

When cooking a whole chicken or turkey, remove accumulated juices from the dish. Otherwise, microwaves will be absorbed by the juices, rather than the bird.

Start a collection of chicken scraps (bones, skin, wing tips, giblets except for liver, etc.) in a labelled bag in the freezer for making broth. Vegetable scraps can be similarly stored.

FILLED BAKED TOMATOES

These colorful tomatoes wear golden hats and are garnished with parsley for an attractive accompaniment to almost any meal. They are delicious with Cornish Hen. To avoid last-minute preparation and hassle, they can be assembled earlier in the day or the night before.

2		large ripe tomatoes	2	
1	tbsp.	butter or margarine	15	mL
1		green onion, finely chopped	1	
1		stalk celery, finely diced	1	
1		slice white bread, diced	1	
1	tbsp.	milk	15	mL
3		soda crackers, finely crushed	3	
1		egg yolk	1	
2	oz.	cooked ham, finely diced	55	g
2	tsp.	ketchup	10	mL
½	tsp.	salt	2	mL
	pinch	pepper	pinch	
1	tsp.	Worcestershire sauce	5	mL
1	dash	Tabasco sauce	1	dash
⅛	tsp.	baking powder	0.5	mL
		cracker crumbs and butter for garnish		
		parsley sprigs		

1. Slice the tops off tomatoes. Scoop out the pulp. Place pulp in a medium-sized bowl. Microwave on **HIGH** for 5 - 6 minutes or until the mixture is very dry.

2. Combine butter, onion and celery in a different bowl. Microwave on **HIGH** for 2 - 3 minutes or until softened. Mix in tomato pulp, bread, milk, crackers and egg yolk. Mix well. A pastry cutter or a potato masher works well.

3. Mix in ham, ketchup, seasonings and baking powder. Microwave on **MEDIUM** for 4 - 5 minutes or until the mixture thickens and moisture evaporates.

4. Fill and mound tomato cups with stuffing. Cover with additional cracker crumbs. Dot with butter. Microwave on **HIGH** for 4 - 5 minutes or until piping hot. Garnish with parsley sprigs.

Serves 2. For 4 servings, double all of the ingredients except the egg. Use 1 whole egg instead of the egg yolk. Double all of the cooking times.

RASPBERRY-YOGURT MOUSSE

A light, yet delicious finale for a special meal. Fresh or frozen berries may be used. Leftovers keep for several days in the refrigerator.

⅓ cup	reconstituted orange juice	75 mL
3 tbsp.	unflavored gelatin (3 envelopes)	45 mL
12 oz.	frozen raspberries	375 mL
⅔ cup	white granulated sugar	150 mL
1 tsp.	orange rind	5 mL
1 cup	plain yogurt	250 mL
3	egg whites	3
1 cup	whipping cream, whipped	250 mL
2 oz.	semisweet chocolate, shaved	55 g

1. Place juice and gelatin in a medium-sized bowl. Microwave on **HIGH** for 2 - 3 minutes or until the mixture just begins to boil. Watch carefully as mixture boils over easily.

2. Place raspberries, sugar and orange rind in a food processor or blender. Purée.

3. Add the dissolved gelatin and process or blend for another 15 seconds. Stir in yogurt.

4. Beat the egg whites until stiff but not dry. Fold into the berry mixture, gently but completely.

5. Spoon mixture into a 1½-quart (1½ L) serving dish. Refrigerate for a few hours before serving.

6. To serve, spoon into dessert dishes and top with a dollop of whipped cream, and chocolate shavings.

Makes 4 servings. To halve, halve all ingredients. Use 2 eggs whites instead of 3. Microwave half of the ingredients for 1 minute.

To achieve a greater volume of beaten egg whites in less time, place egg whites in a microwave-safe bowl and microwave on HIGH for 5 - 7 seconds per egg white. Take care not to over-microwave as they may start to cook slightly around the outside edge, next to the bowl. If you are microwaving any more than 3 egg whites, swirl the mixture after each 15 seconds of microwaving.

VALENTINE'S DAY

CHOCOLATE TIA MARIA COFFEE

This can be partially assembled earlier in the day, and heated when needed. Place dollops of whipped cream on a sheet of waxed paper in the freezer, and avoid last minute preparations.

1 cup	milk	250	mL
1 tsp.	chocolate drink mix	5	mL
1 cup	full-strength coffee	250	mL
3 oz.	Tia Maria	85	mL
2 tbsp.	lemon juice	30	mL
1 tbsp.	white granulated sugar	15	mL
	whipped cream		
1	Skor Chocolate Bar, crushed	1	

1. Place milk, drink mix and coffee in a small bowl. Microwave on **HIGH** for 2 - 3 minutes or until piping hot. Mix in Tia Maria.

2. Dip the rims of 2 coffee cups in lemon juice and then in sugar. Carefully pour the coffee/chocolate mixture into the mugs.

3. Top with a dollop of whipped cream and a heaping tablespoon of crushed Skor Chocolate Bar.

Serves 2. Recipe may be doubled or tripled. Microwave times will double or triple correspondingly.

WHITE CHOCOLATE TRUFFLES

These delicious truffles are a wonderful contrast to the darker chocolate truffles. Flavored with the "love liqueur", Amaretto, these goodies will be a winner with your Valentine.

4 oz.	white chocolate	115	g
¼ cup	butter	50	mL
½ cup	very finely chopped almonds	125	mL
1 tbsp.	Amaretto or Grand Marnier liqueur	15	mL
24	maraschino cherries, well drained	24	
	icing (confectioner's) sugar		

1. Place chocolate in a deep, narrow bowl. Microwave on **HIGH** for 1 - 3 minutes or until the chocolate is almost completely melted.

2. Stir chocolate until it is completely melted. Stir in butter until melted.

3. Stir in nuts and Amaretto. Chill for 2 - 3 hours or until it is firm enough to shape. Shape into 1-inch (2.5 cm) balls, around a cherry. Roll in icing sugar to coat. Store in refrigerator.

Makes 24 truffles.

See photograph page 16A.

CHOCOLATE ALMOND TRUFFLES

These excellent morsels can be frozen for up to a month. Make them well ahead of special occasions. You can find a wide variety of candy cups, made of both foil and paper, in specialty kitchen stores. Adapt the size of the candies to your candy cups for the most attractive look.

6	squares semisweet baking chocolate	6	
⅓ cup	butter or margarine	75	mL
1¼ cups	sifted powder or icing sugar	300	mL
⅔ cup	ground almonds	150	mL
3 tbsp.	milk, rum, or almond liqueur	40	mL
30	whole unblanched almonds	30	
½ cup	chocolate sprinkles	125	mL
½ cup	crushed chocolate wafers (optional)	125	mL
½ cup	ground almonds (optional)	125	mL
½ cup	chopped nuts (optional)	125	mL

1. Melt the chocolate and butter together in a deep, heavy bowl on **HIGH**, uncovered, for 2 - 3 minutes. Stir every minute.

2. Stir together the powdered sugar and the ground almonds.

3. Stir the powdered sugar mixture into the chocolate mixture along with the milk or liqueur. Mix well until blended.

4. Cover and chill mixture until firm enough to shape, about 1 - 2 hours.

5. Use about a rounded teaspoon of mixture for each candy and mold the chocolate mixture around a whole almond, to form a 1-inch ball. If desired, roll balls in the chocolate sprinkles, wafers crumbs, or ground or chopped nuts.

6. Place candies in candy cups or a foil-lined box. Store tightly covered in refrigerator, freezer, or a cool place.

Makes 24 small truffles.

See photograph page 16A.

Going on holidays? Unplug the oven and leave the door slightly ajar. This helps to keep the oven smelling fresh.

To blanch almonds, microwave 1 cup (250 mL) of water on HIGH until it boils. Add ½ cup (125 mL) almonds. Microwave for an additional 30 seconds on HIGH. Drain. Skin almonds.

CHOCOLATE MUD PIE

This delicious recipe is a combination of three of my favorite mud pie recipes. It is a bit "finicky" as each layer has to be chilled thoroughly before the next layer can be added. Be sure to start the evening before, or early the day you wish to serve it. It is worth every minute of time spent.

CRUST:

¼ cup	melted butter or margarine	50 mL
1½ cups	crushed chocolate cookies	375 mL

FILLING:

2½ cups	coffee ice cream	625 mL
15	caramel candies	15
1 tbsp.	milk	15 mL
¼ cup	butter or margarine	50 mL
¼ cup	milk	50 mL
½ cup	white granulated sugar	125 mL
1 cup	semisweet chocolate chips	250 mL
1 cup	whipping cream, whipped, sweetened to taste	250 mL
	chocolate shavings for garnish	

1. Combine crust ingredients and press gently into a large pie plate. Microwave on **HIGH** for 1 minute. Cool completely.

2. Soften ice cream for 1 minute on **DEFROST** or until it can be easily spread into the crumb crust. Spread on the cooled crust.

3. Place in freezer and freeze until the ice cream is once again solid.

4. Place caramels and 1 tbsp. (15 mL) milk in a small bowl. Microwave, uncovered, on **HIGH** for 1 - 1½ minutes or until the caramels can be stirred to a completely smooth mixture. Cool.

5. Pour caramel mixture over frozen ice cream and return to freezer.

6. Place butter, ¼ cup (50 mL) milk and sugar in a medium-sized bowl and microwave for 4 - 5 minutes. Mixture should boil for 3 complete minutes. Stir after 2 minutes.

7. Add chocolate chips to the hot milk mixture and beat until the mixture is thick and glossy looking. Cool slightly. Pour over caramel layer and return to freezer until ½ hour before serving.

8. Pipe the whipped cream onto the top of the pie and garnish with chocolate shavings.

Serves 6.

See photograph page 16A.

CHOCOLATE RUM BROWNIES

Don't wait for Valentine's Day to make these special treats.

2 oz.	unsweetened chocolate	55 g
⅓ cup	butter or margarine	75 mL
2	eggs	2
1 cup	white granulated sugar	250 mL
1 tsp.	vanilla extract	5 mL
⅔ cup	all-purpose flour	150 mL
¼ tsp.	salt	1 mL
½ tsp.	baking powder	2 mL
3 tbsp.	rum	45 mL
	Butter Frosting (below)	
	Chocolate Glaze (page 21)	

1. Place chocolate in a small, microwave-safe bowl. Microwave on **HIGH** for 1 - 2 minutes or until the chocolate is almost completely melted. Stir until completely melted.

2. Beat butter, eggs and sugar together in a large bowl until creamy. Beat in chocolate and vanilla.

3. Combine flour, salt and baking powder in a small bowl, then add to chocolate mixture.

4. Pour into a well-greased 9 x 9-inch (23 x 23 cm) ovenproof glass dish. Cover with a lid or a piece of microwave-safe plastic wrap.

5. Microwave on **MEDIUM HIGH** for 4 - 7 minutes or until the brownies appear dry on the surface, they are starting to pull away from the sides of the dish, and a toothpick inserted in the centre comes out clean.

6. Cool brownies, then sprinkle with rum. Spread with Butter Frosting and top with Chocolate Glaze.

7. Chill; then cut into small squares. Serve chilled.

Makes 3-dozen small brownies.

BUTTER FROSTING

¼ cup	butter or margarine	50 mL
2 cups	icing (confectioner's) sugar	500 mL
1 tsp.	milk	5 mL
1 tsp.	vanilla	5 mL

1. Beat butter and sugar together until creamy. Beat in milk and vanilla, adding just enough milk so that the icing is thick, but spreadable.

2. Spread on cooled brownies and chill to set icing.

Makes 2½ cups of frosting.

CHOCOLATE GLAZE

1 oz.	unsweetened chocolate	30 g
1 tbsp.	butter or margarine	15 mL
¼ cup	light corn syrup	50 mL

1. Melt chocolate and butter together in a deep bowl, on **HIGH** for 1 - 3 minutes, or until chocolate is almost completely melted.

2. Stir until melted. Cool slightly. Stir in corn syrup. Drizzle over butter frosting and spread evenly.

Makes ½ cup of glaze.

PEPPERMINT CHOCOLATE SAUCE

The flavors of chocolate and peppermint are natural companions. This is a real family favorite.

¼ cup	butter or margarine	50 mL
1 cup	white granulated sugar	250 mL
¼ tsp.	salt	1 mL
½ cup	cereal cream	125 mL
6 oz.	unsweetened chocolate, chopped	170 g
3 tbsp.	Crème de menthe	45 mL
½ cup	coarsely crushed peppermint hard candies	125 mL

1. Mix butter, sugar, salt and cream in a deep bowl. Microwave on **HIGH** for 2 - 4 minutes until the sugar is dissolved.

2. Cool mixture for 10 minutes. Stir in chocolate. Stir sauce until chocolate is melted and sauce is smooth. Stir in the Crème de menthe.

3. Serve the sauce warm over chocolate ice cream and sprinkle it with the peppermint candies. The sauce keeps, covered and chilled, for up to 1 week.

Makes 1¾ cups of sauce.

Sugar dissolves faster if warmed before being added to a liquid. Microwave ½ cup (125 mL) of sugar on HIGH for 2 - 3 minutes. Do not over-heat as it scorches easily.

Unsure if your microwave is cooking as fast as it should? Combine 1 cup (250 mL) of water with 8 ice cubes. Stir 2 minutes. Pour off 1 cup (250 mL) of water. Microwave on HIGH until it comes to a boil. For a 625 watt oven the water should come to a boil in approximately 3½ minutes. In a 700 watt output oven the water should boil in approximately 3 minutes.

VIC'S CHOCOLATE FUDGE CAKE

This is a delicious, moist cake. Baked conventionally for genera-
tions in the Dams family, and a tradition at most birthdays, it
microwaves equally well. The recipe can be doubled for a large, 3-
layer cake. As is, it is enough batter for a small 2-layer cake.

½ cup	butter or margarine	125 mL
1¼ cups	white granulated sugar	300 mL
2	eggs	2
1 tsp.	vanilla extract	5 mL
3 tbsp.	cocoa powder	45 mL
1¾ cup	sifted, all-purpose flour	425 mL
⅔ cup	milk	150 mL
1 tsp.	baking soda	5 mL
¾ cup	boiling water	175 mL

1. Beat butter or margarine, sugar and eggs in a large bowl, until light and fluffy. Beat in vanilla.

2. Sift together cocoa and flour. Add dry ingredients alternately with the milk, to the egg mixture, beating well after each addition.

3. Pour soda into the boiling water, and pour this mixture into the batter. Beat until batter is smooth.

4. Pour half of the batter into an 9-inch (23 cm) greased, round dish. Cover with a lid or plate. Microwave on **MEDIUM HIGH** for 5 - 8 minutes or until the cake just starts to pull away from the sides. Do not leave the lid on the cake after it has finished microwaving. A toothpick inserted in the centre of the cake should come out clean.

5. Cool the cake for 5 minutes and then turn out onto a wire cooling rack. Repeat with second half of the batter.

6. Ice with your favorite frosting or the Raspberry Chiffon Topping, page 23.

Serves 8.

Using clear microwave-safe plastic or glass for baking allows a clear view
of the bottom when checking for doneness.

RASPBERRY CHIFFON TOPPING

This delicate pink topping is best spread on a cake about 8 - 12 hours before serving so that the flavors have a chance to blend.

½ cup	raspberry juice concentrate	125 mL
⅓ cup	white granulated sugar	75 mL
2 tbsp.	plain gelatin (2 envelopes)	30 mL
¼ cup	raspberry liqueur*	50 mL
2 cups	whipping cream	500 mL
⅓ cup	white granulated sugar	75 mL
2 tbsp.	raspberry liqueur	30 mL

1. Combine raspberry juice concentrate, sugar (first amount) and gelatin in a medium-sized bowl and microwave on **HIGH** for 2 - 4 minutes. Watch carefully as mixture boils vigorously and may boil over.

2. Stir in first amount of liqueur, cover with wax paper and refrigerate until the mixture is cooled and the consistency of egg whites.

3. Whip cream until soft peaks form, gradually beating in sugar. Fold in the raspberry liqueur mixture. Do not over mix. If you do, the whipping cream becomes very soft and difficult to spread.

4. Sprinkle each cake layer with 1 tbsp. (15 mL) raspberry liqueur. Spread Raspberry Chiffon Topping between layers and on top and sides of cake. Garnish with fresh or frozen raspberries or chocolate shavings.

*Raspberry Liqueur, purchase or make your own, page 121.

Makes 4 cups (1 L) topping.

MOCHA FONDUE

If you prefer a pure chocolate flavor, eliminate the coffee.

1 lb.	semisweet chocolate	500 g
⅛ tsp.	ground cinnamon	0.5 mL
2 tbsp.	strong, liquid coffee	30 mL
⅔ cup	whipping cream	150 mL
1 cup	sifted icing sugar	250 mL

1. Grate chocolate, place in a heavy bowl with cinnamon. Microwave on **HIGH** for 4 - 6 minutes or until chocolate is almost completely melted. Remove from microwave, stir until completely melted.

2. Stir in cream and coffee. Microwave on **HIGH** for an additional 2 - 4 minutes or until mixture is piping hot, but not boiling.

3. Spear bite-sized pieces of oranges, banana, pears, pitted cherries or other fruits, marshmallows, plain cake, with a fondue fork and dip into the chocolate. Dip in icing sugar. Serve with lady fingers.

Serves 4.

SAINT PATRICK'S DAY

The patron saint of Ireland is St. Patrick. He became a monk in France and was given the task by the Pope of converting Ireland to Christianity. He explained the mystery of the Trinity, by showing the Irish a shamrock, which is like a clover, one leaf but three parts. The shamrock is now the emblem of Ireland. March 17th is the anniversary of his death, and this is celebrated as St. Patrick's Day. In Ireland, on St. Patrick's Day, people do not dress up in silly green costumes and parade around in a raucous manner. The North Americans' unique interpretation of this religious holiday is quite different from the way the Irish will celebrate. Ask any Irish traditionalist what they would serve on St. Patrick's Day and every answer might be different. Why not serve up some fun, with the help of the microwave this March 17th.

WHITE STEW

An Irish stew is often made with only white vegetables. It is also different from the Canadian version, as it is cooked in layers.

3 lbs.	lamb chops, fat trimmed, bone removed, cubed	1.5	k
3	medium onions, quartered	3	
6	potatoes, peeled and thinly sliced	6	
1 cup	small mushrooms	250	mL
½ cup	dry white wine	125	mL
2 tbsp.	chopped parsley	30	mL
¼ tsp.	each pepper, thyme, rosemary and marjoram	2	mL
¼ cup	quick-cooking tapioca	50	mL
1 cup	beef stock	250	mL

1. Place the lamb in the bottom of a 3-quart (3 L) casserole and sprinkle with salt and pepper. Layer onions on top of the lamb. Sprinkle with salt and pepper. Top onions with potatoes and mushrooms.

2. Combine remaining ingredients. Pour over meat and vegetables. Cover.

3. Microwave on **LOW** for 2 - 3 hours. This stew requires a long, slow-cooking process, which is accomplished in the microwave by using a low power level. Turnips and celery can be added or substituted.

Serves 4 - 6. Freezes well.

CHAMP

Essentially "champ" is mashed potatoes served in an unusual way. The Irish expression for mashing potatoes is "beetling the champ".

6	medium potatoes	6
¼ cup	water	50 mL
10	green onions	10
½ cup	milk	125 mL
4 tbsp.	butter	60 mL

1. Pierce the potatoes and place all 6 in a 2-quart (2 L) casserole. Add ¼ (50 mL) cup of water, cover, and microwave on **HIGH** for 14 - 18 minutes or until potatoes are just fork tender. Cool slightly.

2. Chop onions finely and add to milk. Microwave onions in milk for 3 - 4 minutes on **MEDIUM** or until onions are just tender.

3. Peel potatoes. Beetle (mash) the champ (potatoes) with milk mixture until light and fluffy. Adjust consistency, by adding more milk.

4. Microwave the butter for 1 - 2 minutes on **HIGH** until it is melted.

5. Place a scoop of potatoes on each plate. Make a hollow in the centre of each mound of potato. Pour the melted butter into each hollow. To eat, dip each forkful of potato into the butter.

Serves 4.

COLCANNON

A tasty dish similar to Champ, made with cabbage.

5	medium potatoes	5
6	green onions, sliced	6
1½ cups	finely chopped raw cabbage	375 mL
½ cup	boiling water	125 mL
1 tbsp.	butter or margarine	15 mL
1 cup	milk	250 mL
1 tbsp.	chopped fresh parsley	15 mL
	salt and pepper to taste	

1. Wash potatoes. Pierce several times with a fork. Microwave on **HIGH**, covered, for 15 - 20 minutes, or until fork tender. Cool slightly and peel.

2. Place onions, cabbage and water in a covered 1-quart (1 L) casserole. Microwave on **HIGH** for 6 - 9 minutes, until cabbage is tender.

3. Toss drained cabbage with butter. Combine potatoes with milk. Beat until light and fluffy. Fold in cabbage, parsley, salt and pepper. Mix well.

Serves 6. To halve recipe, halve all quantities and cooking times.

CHILLED ASPARAGUS WITH GREEN GODDESS DRESSING

There is nothing particularily Irish about asparagus, but it microwaves up to a vivid green color. In March, we are just starting to reap the benefits of a Californian bumper crop. The delicate green dressing is excellent served as a dip as well as a dressing.

1½	lbs.	fresh asparagus	750	g
2	tbsp.	water	30	mL
1	cup	mayonnaise	250	mL
½	cup	watercress leaves	125	mL
3		green onions, sliced	3	
3	tbsp.	chopped parsley	45	mL
3		anchovy fillets	3	
2	tsp.	lemon juice	10	mL
½	tsp.	salt	5	mL
¼	tsp.	white pepper	2	mL
½	cup	sour cream	125	mL
		lettuce		

1. Wash the asparagus and cut off any of the tough or stringy bases.

2. Place asparagus in rectangular dish, as close in size to the asparagus as possible. Arrange the asparagus with half the bases at 1 end and half at the other end. Sprinkle the asparagus with water. Cover the dish with a lid, dinner plate or microwave-safe plastic wrap.

3. Microwave on **HIGH** for 4 - 5 minutes or until the asparagus is just fork tender. Allow to stand for 2 minutes and then retest. If it seems too firm, microwave another 1 - 2 minutes. Drain well. Cool.

4. Combine all of the remaining ingredients, except sour cream and lettuce in a blender and whirl until smooth. Remove from the blender and fold in sour cream. Chill immediately to blend flavors.

5. Line salad plates with lettuce. Lay 4 - 6 spears on each plate. Serve a dollop of dressing on the side.

Serves 4. Since dressing can be stored for up to a week in the refrigerator, recipe can simply be halved by microwaving half as much asparagus.

For chopped hard-cooked egg or a sieved, cooked yolk and white for salad garnish, break an egg into a custard cup, pierce the yolk and cover with microwave-safe plastic wrap. Microwave on LOW for 1 - 1½ minutes or until the yolk is slightly firm, but no longer runny. Let stand several minutes to allow egg to firm before chopping it and adding to salad.

LIME CHIFFON PIE

Top this tasty pie with chocolate shamrocks, see page 30 for recipe. Chiffon Pies are light desserts. This has a refreshing light flavor and a rich texture.

CRUST:

3 tbsp.	butter or margarine	45 mL
2 cups	chocolate wafer crumbs	500 mL
1 tbsp.	white granulated sugar	15 mL

FILLING:

2 tbsp.	unflavored gelatin (2 envelopes)	30 mL
¼ cup	water	50 mL
½ cup	white granulated sugar	125 mL
⅔ cup	freshly squeezed lime juice	150 mL
2 tsp.	grated lime peel	10 mL
4	eggs, separated	4
½ cup	white granulated sugar	125 mL
	chocolate shamrocks, page 30	

1. Melt the butter in a 9-inch (23 cm) pie dish. Add remaining crust ingredients, mix well. GENTLY press the crust on the bottom and sides of the dish.

2. Microwave the crust on **HIGH** for 1 minute. Cool.

3. Dissolve the gelatin in the ¼ cup (50 mL) water. In a medium-sized bowl combine the ½ cup (125 mL) sugar, lime juice and peel. Microwave on **HIGH** for 2 minutes or until the mixture comes to a boil. Add softened gelatin. Microwave for 1 minute more on **HIGH**.

4. Beat egg whites until they form soft peaks. Add the additional ½ cup (125 mL) sugar, slowly, until stiff but not dry.

5. Beat the egg yolks until thick and lemon-colored. Slowly pour lime mixture into the beaten egg yolks, stirring constantly. Cool quickly in freezer or a bowl of ice, until slightly thickened.

6. Fold in the egg whites. Pour into crust. Chill for about three hours or until firm. Just prior to serving garnish with chocolate shamrocks.

Serves 4 - 6. Do not halve.

TIP: The reason for beating the egg whites first is that the beaters do not have to be washed when used in this order.

See photograph page 32A.

IRISH CREAM CAKE

You can use your own homemade Irish Cream Liqueur (see page 29) in this recipe.

¾ cup	chopped pecans	175	mL
19 oz.	golden cake mix, without pudding	520	g
3 oz.	vanilla instant pudding mix	85	g
4	eggs	4	
½ cup	vegetable oil	125	mL
1 cup	Irish Cream Liqueur	250	mL

ICING:

2 cups	icing sugar	500	mL
⅓ cup	butter or margarine	75	mL
¼ tsp.	salt	1	mL
2 tbsp.	Irish Cream Liqueur	30	mL

1. Sprinkle nuts on the bottom of a greased and floured 12 cup (3 L) microwave-safe bundt pan.

2. Combine cake mix, pudding mix, eggs, oil and 1 cup (250 mL) liqueur in a large bowl. Beat until fluffy. Pour batter into prepared bundt pan.

3. Microwave on **MEDIUM**, covered, for 10 - 14 minutes. If the cake is not done, repeat microwaving for 1 minute intervals until it is cooked. When cake is done, a toothpick inserted in the centre will come out clean and the sides of the cake will start to pull away from the bundt pan. Cool and invert pan to release the cake.

4. Combine icing sugar, butter, salt, and 2 tbsp. (30 mL) Irish Cream in a large bowl. Beat, gradually adding the Irish Cream until the desired consistency is achieved.

5. Frost cake. Serve.

Serves 8 - 10, keeps well in refrigerator. Do not halve recipe.

See photograph page 32A.

Nuts toasted in the microwave make an unusual salad garnish. Place 1 cup (500 mL) slivered or sliced almonds or walnut pieces in a single layer in a 9-inch (23 cm) glass pie plate. Microwave on HIGH for 4 - 7 minutes or until nuts are golden brown, stirring every minute.

No ring pan? Place a glass, rim-side down in an 8" (20 cm) round pan, and pour batter around the glass.

IRISH CREAM

A lusty libation is Bailey's Irish Cream, a popular liqueur that you can now simulate with the use of your microwave.

1¾ cup	Irish whiskey	425 mL
1¾ cup	sweetened condensed milk *	425 mL
4	eggs	4
1 cup	whipping cream	250 mL
2 tbsp.	chocolate syrup	30 mL
2 tsp.	instant coffee crystals	10 mL
1 tsp.	vanilla extract	5 mL
½ tsp.	almond extract	2 mL

1. Combine all ingredients in a blender and blend until smooth. Store in the refrigerator in a decanter with a top. Use within a month.

Makes 5 cups (1.25 L).

See photograph page 32A.

* SWEETENED CONDENSED MILK

A simple recipe that you can make yourself. Mixture thickens considerably on standing, so do not over-microwave.

1½ cups	granulated white sugar	375 mL
¼ cup	water	50 mL
⅔ cup	butter, do not substitute	150 mL
2 cups	skim milk, do not substitute	500 mL

1. Mix all ingredients together in a large bowl. If you use too small a bowl the mixture will boil over.

2. Microwave on **HIGH** for 25 - 30 minutes, stirring every 5 minutes or until the mixture is the consistency of a medium sauce. Cool completely.

Makes 1½ - 2 cups. Use in any recipe calling for sweetened condensed milk.

For easier flaming of liquors, preheat in the microwave for 20 seconds/ oz. (20 seconds/30 mL) Do NOT boil. Pour heated liquor over food, and ignite immediately.

CHOCOLATE SHAMROCKS

Using cookie cutters, shapes can be made to suit any occasion.

| 4 oz. | semisweet chocolate | 115 g |
| 1 tbsp. | grated paraffin wax | 15 mL |

1. Microwave chocolate and wax on **HIGH** for 1 - 2 minutes or until the chocolate is almost completely melted. Remove from the microwave and stir until the mixture is completely melted.

2. Spread evenly on a sheet of waxed paper. Let cool until firm. Press a lightly oiled shamrock-shaped cookie cutter sharply into chocolate (or cut around a shamrock pattern).

3. Leave shamrocks on waxed paper and refrigerate until ready to use.

Makes 5 medium-sized shamrocks.

See photograph page 32A.

IRISH COFFEE

As the story goes, Joe Sheridan, a fellow who ran the commissary at Ireland's Shannon Airport concocted this drink as a potion to soothe tired tourists. I wonder if he realized, back in 1949, how very popular this drink would become?

1½ oz.	Irish whiskey	45 mL
½ cup	hot, black brewed coffee	125 mL
1½ tsp.	brown sugar	7 mL
	lightly whipped cream, unsweetened	

1. Place Irish whiskey, coffee and brown sugar into a Irish coffee glass or other suitable footed cup or goblet.

2. Microwave on **HIGH** for 1 - 2 minutes until the mixture is piping hot. DO NOT boil.

3. Pour whipped cream over the back of a spoon so that the cream floats on top. Do not stir.

Serves 1. May be doubled.

To refresh slightly stale coffee beans line a small plate with paper towel. Add 2 tbsp. (30 mL) of beans. Place ½ cup (125 mL) of water beside the beans. Microwave on HIGH for 30 seconds. Shake after 15 seconds to ensure even heating.

No need to grate that hard brown sugar, soften in the microwave quickly and easily. Microwave every 2 cups (500 mL) of brown sugar with 1 slice of bread for 1 - 2 minutes on HIGH or until the brown sugar is softened. Once softened, place in an air-tight container.

EASTER

Long ago in Germany there was a folk tale about a bird who was turned into a rabbit. It was so happy with its new shape that it celebrated its first spring as a bunny by giving people gifts of something it knew how to make when it was a bird: eggs. To this day we love the idea of the bunny bringing eggs at Easter - chocolate and jelly eggs and colored real ones - to celebrate the rebirth of life in the growing-est season of all. Welcome springtime with a parade of exciting Easter treats. From a picture-perfect dinner to surprising desserts and specialties, it's a delicious way to celebrate!

JELLIED EASTER EGGS

This is an unusual idea for Easter eggs, but delightful as a salad at Easter. If you are scrambling eggs for breakfast, don't crack them, read this recipe first.

2x3	oz. pkg.	fruit-flavored gelatin	2x85 g
2½	cups	hot water	625 mL
12		eggs	12

1. Mix gelatin and water together in a small bowl. Microwave on **HIGH** for 4 - 5 minutes or until the mixture just begins to boil. Stir well. Chill until slightly thickened.

2. Using a darning needle or a small skewer, puncture a small hole in the narrow end of each egg; puncture a wider hole in the broad end. Hold egg over bowl and put lips to the small hole; gently blow egg out of the shell into the bowl. Repeat with each egg. Wash shells gently with cold water. Blow all water out of shells. Light a candle and hold over the small hole of each shell, allowing the melting wax to drip over it to seal. Set aside to harden.

3. Pour slightly thickened gelatin into empty egg shells, using a small spoon or a funnel. A large syringe works well, if you have one. Set shells upright in carton and refrigerate at least 3 hours to set. To remove "eggs" crack shells by rolling on a table and peel gently, wetting hands to handle gelatin. Refrigerate until serving time. To serve, arrange on lettuce leaves or a nest of shredded carrots.

Serves 12. Recipe may be easily halved. Use 6 eggs and 1 package of fruit-flavored gelatin.

SCALLOPED POTATOES

The biggest complaint with microwaved scalloped potatoes is that they boil over. I have found that if the potatoes are baked first, then heated in a tasty sauce, the results are more predictable.

6	medium-sized potatoes	6
2 tbsp.	butter or margarine	30 mL
2 tbsp.	all-purpose flour	30 mL
½ tsp.	salt	2 mL
1 tbsp.	dry onion flakes	30 mL
1 tsp.	Worcestershire sauce	5 mL
½ tsp.	dry mustard	2 mL
⅛ tsp.	freshly ground pepper	1 mL
1 cup	milk	250 mL
1 cup	grated Cheddar cheese	250 mL
½ cup	buttered bread crumbs (optional)	125 mL

1. Pierce potatoes with a fork. Microwave on **HIGH** for 18 minutes or until the potatoes are just starting to soften. Do not overcook, or the scalloped potatoes will become mushy.

2. Place butter in a small bowl. Microwave on **HIGH** for 1 minute or until melted. Stir in flour and spices. Slowly mix in milk. Microwave on **HIGH** for 2 - 3 minutes, stirring every 30 seconds, until thickened.

3. Stir in the cheese. Mix until it is melted. Slice the potatoes thinly. Place in a 2-quart (2 L) casserole. Pour sauce over the potatoes. Top with buttered bread crumbs. Microwave on **MEDIUM HIGH** for 4 - 5 minutes or until the potatoes are completely softened and the sauce is bubbly.

4. Let stand for 2 - 3 minutes before serving.

Serves 4 - 5. Can be halved. Microwave 2 potatoes for 8 minutes. Prepare half of the amount of sauce. Microwave the prepared casserole for 2 - 3 minutes on MEDIUM HIGH.

BROCCOLI AND HERBS

A simple recipe that is very tasty.

1½ lbs.	broccoli	750 g
¼ cup	butter or margarine	50 mL
¼ cup	lemon juice	50 mL
¼ tsp.	garlic powder	1 mL
¼ tsp.	salt	1 mL
¼ tsp.	ground black pepper	1 mL
¼ tsp.	oregano	1 mL
¼ tsp.	sweet basil	1 mL
¼ tsp.	tarragon	1 mL

SAINT PATRICK'S DAY

Tablecloth hand-made by Jenny Dams

BROCCOLI AND HERBS (cont'd.)

1. Wash broccoli. Cut the tough bottoms off the stems. Place broccoli in a medium-sized bowl. Cover. Microwave on **HIGH** for 5 - 7 minutes or until the broccoli is bright green in color, and fork tender.

2. Melt butter on **HIGH** for 1 - 2 minutes. Add remaining ingredients. Microwave on **HIGH** for an additional 1 minute. Pour over broccoli.

Serves 6. Recipe may be halved. The butter is also tasty over cauliflower, zucchini, asparagus and green beans.

JENNY'S BEAN SALAD

The first time I met my mother-in-law she was busy preparing this salad. It has since become one of my favorites, and she one of my favorite mother-in-laws!

16 oz.	canned red kidney beans	500 g
16 oz.	fresh or frozen yellow beans	500 g
16 oz.	fresh or frozen green beans	500 g
1	medium onion, sliced and separated into rings	1
¼ cup	vinegar	50 mL
½ cup	salad oil	125 mL
¼ tsp.	sugar	1 mL
¼ tsp.	salt	1 mL
¼ tsp.	pepper	1 mL
¼ tsp.	dried mustard	1 mL
pinch	each of thyme, basil and garlic	pinch

1. Drain kidney beans. Set aside. Place washed, trimmed and cut green and yellow beans in a small, microwave-safe casserole. Sprinkle with ½ cup (125 mL) water.

2. Microwave on **HIGH** for 5 - 6 minutes or until the beans are tender crisp. Place onion rings on top of the beans and microwave for an additional 3 minutes on **HIGH** until the beans are tender. The onions should still be firm. Drain well. Cool.

3. Add the drained vegetables to the kidney beans. Combine remaining ingredients; pour over beans and toss well. Cover and chill several hours or overnight.

Serves 8 - 10.

Substituting chicken, beef or vegetable broth for the water when cooking vegetables gives them a much richer flavor.

ASPARAGUS DIVINE

A delicious casserole that can be prepared ahead of time and heated when needed.

2	lbs.	fresh asparagus	1 kg
1	cup	sliced mushrooms	250 mL
3	tbsp.	butter or margarine	45 mL
3	tbsp.	all-purpose flour	45 mL
1	tsp.	salt	5 mL
¼	tsp.	pepper	1 mL
1½	cups	milk	375 mL
¾	cup	slivered, toasted almonds	175 mL
¾	cup	grated cheese	175 mL

1. Trim the tough bottoms off the asparagus. Wash. Place asparagus in a rectangular dish, as close in size to the asparagus as possible. Arrange the asparagus with half the bases at 1 end and half at the other end. Sprinkle the asparagus with water. Cover the dish with a lid, plate or a microwave-safe plastic wrap.

2. Microwave on **HIGH** for 6 - 8 minutes or until the asparagus is tender-crisp. Drain. Set aside.

3. Place mushrooms and butter in a small bowl. Microwave on **HIGH** for 2 minutes or until the mushrooms are tender. Blend in flour, salt and pepper and mix well. Slowly add milk and stir until there are no lumps.

4. Microwave on **MEDIUM HIGH** for 2 - 4 minutes until the sauce thickens. Stir every 30 seconds.

5. Place drained asparagus in a 1½-quart (1.5 L) casserole. Spread sauce over asparagus. Top with almonds, and cheese.

6. Microwave on **HIGH** for 2 - 4 minutes or until the cheese is melted and the milk sauce bubbly. If the casserole has been refrigerated, microwave for 4 - 6 minutes on **MEDIUM HIGH**.

Serves 4 - 6. Recipe may be halved. Halve all ingredients and cooking times.

If you are unsure of the wattage of your oven, measure exactly 1 L of water into a microwave-safe bowl, then record the temperature in °C. Microwave on HIGH for exactly 1 minute. Record the temperature in °C. The difference of the 2 temperatures multiplied by 70 will give you the approximate wattage of your microwave oven.

LEG OF LAMB PERSILE

I am so often asked if lamb can be microwaved. This delicious recipe is a perfect example of just how versatile the microwave is.

5 - 6 lbs.	leg of lamb, fell removed*	2 - 3	kg
2	cloves of garlic, crushed	2	
	salt and pepper		
3 tbsp.	lemon juice or vinegar	45	mL
4 cups	fresh bread crumbs	1	L
1 cup	finely chopped parsley	250	mL
1 tsp.	thyme	5	mL
¾ cup	butter or margarine	175	mL
	fresh parsley sprigs		

1. Rub the lamb with garlic, salt and pepper. Sprinkle with lemon juice. The lemon juice will season the lamb and lessen the cooking aroma. Cover with waxed paper.

2. Combine bread crumbs, chopped parsley and thyme with melted butter and set aside until 10 minutes before the roast is finished cooking.

3. Microwave lamb roast for 11 minutes/lb. (24 minutes/kg) on **MEDIUM**. If you are using a probe, insert the probe into the centre of the leg and microwave on **MEDIUM** until the internal temperature reaches 150°F (65°C). Approximately 10 minutes before the roast has finished cooking, remove it from the microwave.

4. Press the parsley-crumb mixture firmly on the top and sides of the leg, covering completely. Return lamb to the microwave for the remainder of the cooking time. The coating should be a golden brown.

5. Let the lamb stand for 10 minutes, covered, prior to carving. After the lamb has been carved, garnish with parsley sprigs.

Serves 6 - 8.

* The fell is the thin outer covering of the lamb leg.

If you notice that the narrow end of the leg of lamb is over cooking, completely cover with a piece of foil for the remainder of the cooking time.

To dry bread for crumbs or toppings place 2 slices of bread on a paper towel and microwave on HIGH for 90 seconds - 2 minutes. Let stand 2 minutes to complete the drying process.

STRAWBERRY PIE

I was amazed at the popularity and exhorbitant price of fresh strawberry pie while visiting in Los Angeles last spring. Determined to match the delicious flavor, at less cost, I came up with this recipe and 5 extra pounds on my hips! It's delicious, and really a super treat this time of year. Use only fresh strawberries.

CRUST:

1½ cups	all-purpose flour	375 mL
½ cup	butter	125 mL
1	egg yolk	1
½ tsp.	salt	2 mL
2½ - 3 tbsp.	cold water	40 - 50 mL

1. Mix flour, butter, egg yolk and salt together with fingers until coarse and crumbly. Add cold water until a ball forms. Dough may also be mixed in a food processor. Knead for 2 minutes. Wrap in waxed paper. Chill for 30 minutes.

2. Roll out the dough, line a 9-inch (23 cm) glass plate, prick lightly with a fork, flute the edges and chill again until firm.

3. Microwave on **HIGH** for 4 - 6 minutes or until flaky. Cool.

FILLING:

2 tbsp.	butter	30 mL
¼ cup	all-purpose flour	50 mL
1¼ cups	milk	300 mL
2 tbsp.	white granulated sugar	30 mL
1	egg yolk	1
1 tbsp.	light cream	15 mL
1 tbsp.	sweet sherry (optional)	15 mL
1½ cups	strawberries	375 mL
4 tbsp.	strawberry jam	60 mL
1 tbsp.	lemon juice	15 mL
	whipped cream for serving	

Always stir food that is being cooked in the microwave from the outside of the dish to the center.

STRAWBERRY PIE (cont'd.)

1. Microwave butter in a medium-sized bowl on **HIGH** for 1 minute or until it is completely melted.

2. Add the flour and mix well. Gradually stir in the milk and microwave on **HIGH** for 2 - 3 minutes or until the mixture thickens and just comes to a boil. Stir every 30 seconds.

3. Whisk in the sugar, egg yolk, cream and sherry until smooth. Microwave for 1 minute on **HIGH**.

4. Pour into the baked pastry shell and allow to cool.

5. Hull the strawberries, except for 4 or 5 to be used for decoration and arrange them whole or halved over the cooled filling.

6. Prepare the glaze by microwaving the jam on **HIGH** for 1 minute. Stir in the lemon juice. Cool slightly and pour or brush over the strawberries. Chill until set. At serving time, after cutting each piece, serve with a dollop of whipped cream.

Serves 6 - 8. Recipe cannot be easily halved.

To soften or warm corn or flour tortillas, place 6 between damp paper towels. Microwave on HIGH for 30 - 45 seconds.

How do you know when a plate of heated food is hot enough to serve? When the center bottom feels warm to the touch.

Soften hard-frozen ice cream for easy serving. Microwave on LOW for 30 - 45 seconds per pint (500 mL) until soft enough to scoop.

MICROWAVED HAM

No matter how you slice it, ham heats up nicely in the microwave. Since most hams, boneless and bone-in, are fully cooked, they only require heating to serving temperature. Although it is possible to cook a whole or half ham in most microwave ovens, the results are usually better and quicker if hams more than 3 - 4 lbs. (2 kg) are sliced or carved before microwaving.

Ham is compact and dense and is more resistant to microwave penetration than most other meats. When whole hams weighing over 5 lbs.(2.5 kg) are microwaved, muscles separate and the outside portions may become dry before the center reaches serving temperature.

MICROWAVING FULLY COOKED HAM UNDER 4 LBS. (2 KG)

Place the ham on a plate, or a roasting rack. If you have a probe, insert the probe into a meaty portion of the ham, away from bone or fat Microwave on **MEDIUM** until the internal temperature of the meat reaches 140°F (60°C). Let the ham stand 10 minutes before carving. If you do not have a probe, microwave for 4 - 6 minutes per lb. (9 - 13 minutes/kg). Check the internal temperture of the ham prior to carving. It should be no less than 140°F (60°C). A glaze may be applied during the last few minutes of cooking. Do not add sooner, or the glaze may scorch.

MICROWAVING FULLY COOKED HAM SLICES

Slicing or carving a large ham and overlapping or stacking slices in micro-wave-safe dishes speeds heating and results in juicy tender meat.

Place ham slices in microwave-safe dish, cover with waxed paper and microwave on **MEDIUM** 8 minutes / lb. (17 minutes/ kg) or until the internal temperature reaches 140°F (60°C).

RAW HAM

Place the ham in a cooking bag such as "LOOK" or "ROAST AND BOAST". Arrange in baking dish so cut side will be to the front of the oven. Tie the bag closed. Make an x-shaped slash near closure. Insert probe through bag into the centre of the ham. Microwave on **MEDIUM** until the internal temperature reaches 160° (71°C). Let stand 10 minutes before carving. If you do not have a probe, microwave the ham on **MEDIUM** for 12 - 15 minutes per lb. (25 - 30 minutes / kg), in a plastic bag.

PLUM GLAZE OR SAUCE

A delicious glaze that can be added during the last 10 minutes of baking. Any extra glaze may be passed as a sauce.

12 oz.	plum jam	365	mL
⅓ cup	rose wine	75	mL
1	lemon, juice and rind	1	
1 tbsp.	red wine vinegar	15	mL
1 tbsp.	ketchup	15	mL
1 tsp.	ground ginger	5	mL
¾ tsp.	fennel seed, crushed	3	mL
½ tsp.	ground cinnamon	2	mL
⅛ tsp.	ground cloves	0.5	mL
1 tbsp.	grated onion	15	mL
1	clove garlic	1	
2 - 3	drops Tabasco sauce	2 - 3	

1. Combine all ingredients in a a medium-sized bowl. Microwave on **MEDIUM** for 4 - 6 minutes or until the preserves have melted. Spoon over ham during the last 5 minutes of microwaving.

2. Leftover glaze may be passed as a sauce when serving ham.

Makes 2 cups (500 mL) of glaze or enough for a 3 - 4 lb. (2 kg) ham.

PINEAPPLE MUSTARD SAUCE

Serve warm. Wonderful with ham, roast pork or duck.

8 oz.	crushed pineapple	250	mL
2 tbsp.	white granulated sugar	30	mL
1 tbsp.	cornstarch	15	mL
1 tbsp.	dry mustard	15	mL
¼ tsp.	salt	1	mL
3 tbsp.	prepared mustard	45	mL
10 - 12	maraschino cherries, sliced	10 - 12	

1. Drain juice from crushed pineapple and add enough water or orange juice to measure exactly 1 cup (250 mL) of liquid.

2. Combine sugar, cornstarch, dry mustard and salt in a small bowl. Gradually stir in pineapple juice. Microwave on **HIGH** for 2 - 3 minutes, stirring every 30 seconds, or until the mixture is thick and clear.

3. Add prepared mustard, pineapple and cherry slices if using. Microwave on **HIGH** for an additional minute to heat through. Serve warm.

Makes enough for 4 - 6 servings, and will keep for 2 - 3 weeks in the refrigerator.

SAUCY RAISINS

Although excellent with ham, it is also a fine accompaniment for sandwiches made from leftover ham.

3 cups	raisin pie filling (recipe follows)	750 mL
½ cup	packed brown sugar	125 mL
½ tsp.	dry mustard	2 mL
¼ tsp.	ground ginger	1 mL
3 tbsp.	cider vinegar	45 mL
½ tsp.	Worcestershire sauce	2 mL

1. Combine all ingredients in a large bowl and microwave on **HIGH** for 3 - 4 minutes or until heated through. Serve with roast pork or ham.

Makes 4 cups of sauce. May be halved.

RAISIN PIE FILLING

2 cups	seedless raisins	500 mL
2 cups	water	500 mL
½ cup	sugar	125 mL
¼ tsp.	salt	1 mL
¼ cup	butter or margarine	50 mL
¼ cup	flour	50 mL
1 tbsp.	rum (optional)	15 mL

1. In a medium-sized bowl, combine raisins and water. Microwave on **HIGH** for 3 - 4 minutes or until mixture comes to a boil.

2. Stir in sugar and salt. In a small bowl, cream butter and flour until it forms a paste. Gently stir into raisin mixture. Microwave on **MEDIUM** for 2 - 4 minutes stirring gently every 30 seconds until the mixture has thickened.

Makes enough filling for a 9-inch pie.

It is possible to quickly soften dried fruit, that has hardened, using the microwave. For every ½ cup (125 mL) of dried fruit add 1 - 2 tsp. (5 - 10 mL) of water or rum. Microwave, covered on HIGH for 30 - 45 seconds. Rum imparts a unique flavor to the fruit which is delicious in baked products.

BAKED BRANDIED PEACHES

My mother used to serve these with ham as part of the main course and we all enjoyed the change from the more traditional pineapple glazes. They are also popular spooned over ice cream, or an unfrosted cake.

4	peaches	4	
¼ cup	butter	50	mL
½ cup	packed brown sugar	125	mL
¼ cup	brandy	50	mL
¼ tsp.	cinnamon	1	mL
⅛ tsp.	nutmeg	0.5	mL

1. Peel and pit peaches. Slice, quarter or halve and arrange evenly in the bottom of a 9-inch (23 cm) pie dish.

2. Combine butter, sugar, brandy and spices in a small microwave-safe bowl. Microwave on **HIGH** for 1 - 2 minutes or until the butter is melted.

3. Pour the butter mixture over the peaches. Microwave on **MEDIUM** for 10 - 15 minutes, basting twice, until the peaches are tender. Rearrange the peaches if they are softening too much in one area.

Serves 4. Recipe may be halved. Halve all ingredients. Microwave peaches and butter sauce for 7 minutes on MEDIUM.

To avoid boil-overs with liquid foods such as soups and sauces, use a container two- or three- times larger than the amount you are cooking.

If your microwave needs freshening, and even the dog hides when you open it, squeeze the juice of 1 lemon in 4 cups (1 L) of hot water. Microwave on HIGH for 10 - 30 minutes (depending on how bad it smells). Your oven will remain fresh smelling for months! As an added bonus, any baked-on spills will wipe away much easier once the lemon water has been boiled in the microwave oven.

MOTHER'S DAY

Being a mother, I can't think of a more fitting way to celebrate the day, and do something special for Mom than prepare a meal for her. Pamper her with affection and treat her to a delicious brunch. It's easier than you think, as easy as A.B.C. if you plan ahead, work together and follow the detailed instruction given in this section. It's important to plan ahead for any dinner. Make sure you have all the ingredients on hand before you start. Decide which dishes take the longest to prepare or which ones can be made in advance and refrigerated, and start those first. Divide the work if necessary. My mother's favorite recipe for chicken is given in this section, as well as my favorite dessert recipe. Enjoy - show her how much you love her!

EGGS BENEDICT FOR 4

This isn't as difficult as you may think.

		butter or margarine	
8		medium-sized eggs	8
8		slices of back bacon	8
4		English Muffins, traditional	4
1	recipe	Hollandaise Sauce, recipe to follow	
		parsley or paprika for garnish	

NOTE: If you have 8 ovenproof glass custard cups, they work perfectly for this recipe; however if you don't, 1 of the following 3 things would be suitable:

(1) Some short, durable, wide-mouthed juice glasses (they will need to measure about 3 inches (7.5cm) across the top);

(2) Paper cups, measuring 3 inches (7.5 cm) across the top;

(3) Microwave muffin tins that don't have holes in the bottom.

1. Rub a little butter or margarine on the inside of each cup or glass with a piece of paper towel. Carefully break 1 egg into each cup. Take a fork and carefully poke the white of each egg several times. Place the eggs in the microwave in a large circle on the floor of the oven. If you have a muffin tin you will notice that the eggs are already arranged in a circular shape.

2. Microwave 8 eggs on **DEFROST** for 6- 9 minutes. Do not use Jet Defrost or Auto Defrost if you have these. Use **POWER LEVEL 3** or **LOW** and NOT the Auto or Jet Defrost setting.

EGGS BENEDICT FOR 4 (cont'd.)

3. Open microwave and look at the eggs after 5 minutes. Some of them may be less cooked than others. Take the less cooked eggs and put them in the spot where the more completely cooked eggs are, take those eggs and put them where the less cooked eggs were. Give each dish a half turn. If you are using a muffin tin, give the entire muffin tin a half-turn.

4. Microwave on **DEFROST** for an additional 3 - 4 minutes or until the whites are completely white. Do not overcook or the yolk will set.

5. Remove eggs from microwave, and cover with a clean tea towel to keep warm. While eggs are microwaving, place bacon slices on a pie plate or a dinner plate that is microwave-safe. Once you have removed the eggs, the bacon can be put in the oven. There is no need to cover. Microwave on **HIGH** for 4 minutes or until the bacon is sizzling hot.

6. While the bacon is microwaving you can start toasting the muffins. Split each muffin in half, and place one half in each side of the toaster. After each muffin is toasted, butter it and place on a plate and cover with a tea towel to keep warm.

7. Prepare Hollandaise Sauce. To assemble: place 2 muffin halves on each plate and then put a slice of back bacon on each muffin. Carefully slide 1 egg on each. Pour about 2 tbsp. (30 mL) of Hollandaise Sauce over each half. Sprinkle with paprika or parsley. Serve immediately.

Serves 4. If you want fewer, adjust recipe quantities as follows. For each person you will need 2 eggs, 2 pieces of back bacon and 1 English muffin. The Hollandaise Sauce should NOT be altered. Your timings will also vary. As a general rule, each egg will require slightly more than one minute of microwaving on DEFROST. Each piece of back bacon will require 40 seconds to 1 minute on HIGH.

HOLLANDAISE SAUCE

¾ cup	butter	175 mL
2 tbsp.	water	30 mL
3	egg yolks	3
1 tbsp.	lemon juice	15 mL
	pinch of dry mustard	

1. Melt butter, whisk in water, egg yolks, lemon juice and dry mustard.

2. Microwave on **MEDIUM HIGH** 30 seconds at a time, whisk after each interval, until sauce thickens slightly. Do not overcook, sauce will curdle.

Makes 1¼ cup of sauce. Do NOT halve recipe.

ELEGANT OMELET

Omelets can be easily microwaved, and then filled with your favorite fillings.

1 tbsp.	butter or margarine	15 mL	
4	eggs, separated	4	
¼ cup	milk	50 mL	
½ tsp.	salt	2 mL	
dash	pepper	1 mL	

OMELET FILLINGS:

chopped ham and cheese
cooked shrimp or crabmeat
chopped artichoke hearts
crumbled bacon
Cheddar cheese, grated
picante (hot) sauce
sautéed mushrooms
sautéed onions

1. Melt butter in a 9-inch (23 cm) pie plate. Mix together yolks, milk, salt and pepper. Beat egg whites until stiff. Fold yolks into whites with a spatula. Pour into pie plate, leveling mixture. Cover with a lid or pie plate.

2. Microwave on **HIGH** for 4 - 6 minutes. Omelet should be almost completely set through. Don't microwave until the eggs are completely set.

3. Place filling or fillings of your choice on half of the omelet. Slip a long spatula under the unfilled side - lift and flip over to cover filling. Cut omelet into 3 or 4 wedges.

Serve 3 - 4. Serve with hot buttered toast or English Muffins.

GRAND MARNIER GRAPEFRUIT

You may balk at the thought of warmed grapefruit. It has an enhanced flavor. Perhaps the Grand Marnier helps?

2	large, firm grapefruit	2	
4 tbsp.	Grand Marnier	60 mL	
4 tbsp.	brown sugar	60 mL	
4 tsp.	softened butter	20 mL	
4	maraschino cherries	4	

GRAND MARNIER GRAPEFRUIT (cont'd.)

1. Cut the grapefruit in half. Carefully cut around each section of the fruit, so that the sections can be removed easily.

2. Drizzle 1 tbsp. (15 mL) of Grand Marnier over each half. Sprinkle each half with ¼ of the brown sugar and butter. Top with cherry.

3. Place each half on a small microwave-safe plate. Microwave all 4 halves for 2 - 3 minutes on **HIGH** until just warmed through. Serve warm.

Serves 4. Recipe is easily adjusted for more or fewer servings. Microwave each half on HIGH for 30 - 45 seconds.

SHRIMP AND CRAB QUICHE

A quiche cooks quickly and evenly if covered when microwaving. Cook pastry shell before adding uncooked filling. Microwave, or for a golden color, prebake conventionally.

9- inch	cooked pastry shell	23	cm
1 cup	grated Swiss cheese	250	mL
½ lb.	crabmeat, cooked, drained	250	g
½ lb.	shrimp, cooked, deveined	250	g
2	green onions, finely chopped	2	
4	large eggs, beaten	4	
1 cup	evaporated milk	250	mL
1 tbsp.	ketchup	15	mL
½ tsp.	salt	2	mL
⅛ tsp.	cayenne	0.5	mL
	parsley for garnish		

1. Spread the cheese evenly over the bottom of the cooled pie shell. Top with crabmeat and shrimp.

2. Place green onion in a small cup or bowl. Microwave on **HIGH** for 2 - 3 minutes or until soft. Sprinkle onion over crab and shrimp.

3. Mix beaten eggs, evaporated milk, ketchup, salt and cayenne until light and airy. Pour carefully over the ingredients in the bottom of the pie shell. Cover with a lid or plate.

4. Microwave on **MEDIUM HIGH** for 7 - 9 minutes or until the quiche is set but still jiggles slightly in the center. Let stand for 2 - 3 minutes.

Serves 6. Recipe may be halved. Prepare the quiche in a 6-inch (9 cm) casserole dish or quiche dish if you have one. Halve all ingredients, cover and microwave on MEDIUM HIGH for 4 - 6 minutes.

MOM'S PARMESAN CHICKEN

This is a very easy chicken dish to prepare, and one that has always been a favorite in our house. The recipe is originally my mother's, but her version, like so many great recipes, was prepared with a pinch of this and a shake of that. As near as I can tell, these are the quantities that she uses.

3 lbs.	chicken pieces	1.5 kg
¾ cup	dry, white wine	175 mL
3 tbsp.	butter or margarine	45 mL
1	clove garlic, minced	1
1 cup	dry bread crumbs	250 mL
⅓ cup	Parmesan cheese	75 mL
	salt and pepper	

1. Wash chicken pieces, pat dry, and place in the bottom of a 2-quart (2L) casserole. Sprinkle with wine.

2. Combine butter or margarine and garlic, in a small bowl. Microwave on **HIGH** for 2 minutes or until the garlic just begins to turn golden brown. Pour butter over the bread crumbs. Mix well.

3. Sprinkle bread crumbs over the chicken. Top with Parmesan cheese. Sprinkle with salt and pepper if desired. Cover.

4. Microwave on **HIGH** for 15 minutes. Remove cover. Continue microwaving for 4 - 8 minutes or until the chicken is tender and juices run clear. Do NOT undercook. There should be no pink meat remaining.

Serves 6 persons. Recipe may be halved. Halve all ingredients. Microwave for 8 minutes on HIGH, covered. Remove cover and continue microwaving for 3 - 6 minutes or until the meat is no longer pink.

See photograph page 48A.

MAPLE-GLAZED CARROTS

These tasty carrots are excellent with any type of chicken dish.

4	medium carrots	4
¼ cup	water	50 mL
2 tbsp.	maple syrup	30 mL
1 tbsp.	butter	15 mL
½ tsp.	salt	2 mL
	dried mint, or chopped fresh	

1. Wash and peel carrots. Slice evenly into coins. Place in a 2-cup (500 mL) casserole. Add water. Cover tightly and microwave on **HIGH** for 4 - 6 minutes or until the carrots are tender but firm.

MAPLE-GLAZED CARROTS (cont'd.)

2. In a separate bowl, mix maple syrup, butter and salt. Mix in liquid from the cooked carrots. Pour this mixture over the carrots.

3. Microwave the carrots, uncovered, for 2 - 3 more minutes or until they are evenly glazed and the carrots are tender. Garnish with mint and serve.

Serves 6. Recipe may be halved. Halve ingredients and microwave on HIGH for 2 - 3 minutes without the glaze. Glaze and microwave for an additional 1 - 2 minutes.

RICE PILAF

Rice is fantasic when microwaved properly. If you anticipate using the microwave during the hectic dinner time, prepare the rice early in the day, and reheat to a just-cooked flavor just prior to serving.

3 tbsp.	butter	45 mL
1 cup	finely chopped onion	250 mL
1½ cups	uncooked, long grain rice	375 mL
2½ cups	chicken stock	625 mL
2 tbsp.	fresh parsley, cut	30 mL
1	bay leaf	1
¼ tsp.	thyme	1 mL
1 tsp.	salt	5 mL
¼ tsp.	white pepper	1 mL
½ cup	dry white wine	125 mL

1. Microwave 2 tbsp. (30 mL) butter and onion in a 2-quart (2L)* micro-wave-safe casserole on **HIGH** for 6 minutes, or until the onion is tender and transparent. Add rice. Microwave on **HIGH** for an additional 2 minutes.

2. Add stock, herbs, spices** and wine. Cover with a lid and microwave on **HIGH** for 20 minutes. Stir halfway through the cooking time. Let stand, covered, 10 minutes. Remove the bay leaf.

3. Dot rice with remaining butter, stir with a fork to fluff rice. Adjust seasonings if necessary.

   * Make sure you use a large dish for microwaving the rice. It boils vigorously in the microwave and will boil over if a smaller dish is used.

   **Eliminate the salt if you are using dry chicken base to make the chicken stock. The dried base mixes contain plenty of salt.

Serves 6 persons ½ cup (125 mL) each. Do not halve recipe. Rice freezes and refrigerates well.

See photograph page 48A.

BANANA CREAM PIE

This delicious pie is easy and perfect for kids to prepare for Mom's special day.

CRUST:

2	cups	vanilla wafer crumbs	500	mL
2	tbsp.	melted butter or margarine	30	mL
2	tbsp.	white granulated sugar	30	mL

FILLING:

⅔	cup	white granulated sugar	150	mL
3½	tbsp.	cornstarch	50	mL
½	tsp.	salt	5	mL
2	cups	milk	500	mL
3		beaten egg yolks	3	
1	tbsp.	butter	15	mL
1½	tsp.	vanilla	7	mL
3		bananas	3	
1	cup	whipped cream	250	mL

1. Mix together crust ingredients until crumbly. Press gently into the bottom of a 9-inch (23 cm) pie dish. Microwave on **HIGH** for 2 minutes or until slightly firm. Cool.

2. Mix sugar, cornstarch and salt in the bottom of a 2-quart (2L) glass bowl. Stir in milk until evenly mixed. Microwave on **HIGH** for 8-10 minutes, stirring every 2 minutes. Microwave until the mixture is boiling and thickened.

3. Stir a small amount of the hot liquid into the eggs and then return the egg mixture to the hot liquid. Microwave on **HIGH** for 2 - 3 minutes, stirring once.

4. Add butter and vanilla. Cool slightly.

5. Slice bananas thinly and place in an even layer in the bottom of the pie crust. Pour cooled filling over bananas. When cool, garnish with whipped cream.

Serves 6. Do not halve recipe.

For a quick creamy fruit dressing, soften 1 cup (250 mL) of strawberry or peach ice cream on HIGH for 45 - 60 seconds and fold in 1 cup (250 mL) mayonnaise. Stir in ⅛ tsp. (0.5 mL) curry powder, nutmeg or allspice.

MOTHER'S DAY

Clockwise From Foreground
1. Asparagus with Sesame-Soy Dressing, page 61
2. Rice Pilaf, page 47
3. Mom's Parmesan Chicken, page 46
4. Krispie Tartlets, page 49
5. Spinach Salad with Poppy Seed Dressing, page 13

KRISPIE TARTLETS

Here's a different way to prepare an all-time favorite. This can be made early in the day and refrigerated until dessert time.

2 tbsp.	butter or margarine	30 mL
20	large marshmallows	20
2½ cups	Rice Krispies	625 mL

FILLING:

2 cups	frozen strawberries	500 mL
1 cup	juice from berries plus water	250 mL
3 oz.	strawberry flavored gelatin	85 g
1 tbsp.	unflavored gelatin (1 envelope)	15 mL
6 oz.	frozen orange juice concentrate	170 g
⅓ cup	cold water	75 mL
2 cups	vanilla ice cream, softened	500 L

1. Microwave butter in a large bowl on **HIGH** for 30 seconds or until it is completely melted.

2. Add marshmallows. Microwave on **HIGH** for 2 - 3 minutes, stirring every 30 seconds until the marshmallows are melted and the mixture is smooth.

3. Remove from the microwave, add Rice Krispies and mix until they are evenly coated.

4. Butter 24 muffin cups, 2¾ inch (7 cm) size. Put about 1 heaping tablespoon (14 mL) of Rice Krispie mixture into each cup. Press around sides to form shells. Chill.

5. Drain the berries. Add enough water to the juice to yield 1 cup (250 mL). Microwave 1 cup (250 mL) of the berry juice with the gelatins, for 2 - 3 minutes on **HIGH** or until the gelatin is dissolved. Do not boil.

6. Stir in orange juice concentrate and cold water. Add softened ice cream and blend. Fold in fruit. Spoon enough of the mixture into each Rice Krispie cup, so that it is mounded. Chill until ready to serve.

7. To serve: remove the tarts from the muffin tins and place 1 or 2 on a plate for each person.

Serves 8 - 10. Recipe keeps for several days in the refrigerator. Can be halved.

See photograph page 48A.

FATHER'S DAY

A once-a-year chance to make something just for Dad. All of the recipes are more to most Dad's liking - hearty. Designed to suit Dad's tastes, these recipes can all be made early in the day and reheated just before supper. Gives all proud kids a chance to sit and watch a ball-game with Dad, or go for an afternoon of fishing. Look over the recipes and adapt the preparation time to your plans for the day.

CAJUN-STYLE RED SNAPPER

This recipe requires a browning dish or a cast-iron skillet on top of the stove. It is an excellent recipe and definitely lifts ordinary-flavored fish to EXTRA-ordinary.

1 tbsp.	plain dry bread crumbs	15 mL
1 tsp.	dried basil	5 mL
1 tsp.	paprika	5 mL
½ tsp.	fennel seeds	2 mL
½ tsp.	dried thyme	2 mL
½ tsp.	dried oregano	2 mL
½ tsp.	salt	2 mL
½ tsp.	freshly ground pepper	2 mL
¼ tsp.	red pepper flakes	1 mL
2 - 5 oz.	red snapper fillets	2-140 g
½	lime	½

1. Preheat browning tray for maximum time allowed (8 minutes for a medium-sized browning skillet). If using a frying pan instead of the browning skillet, heat until very hot.

2. Grind crumbs with all ingredients except fillet and lime in a food processor or blender until fine. Coat fillets with crumbs.

3. Place fish in preheated browning dish or frying pan. Press down firmly with a spatula. Let brown for 1 minute, turn fish over. Press again. Fish should be crisp, golden and slightly blackened in spots.

4. Place the browning dish back in the microwave and microwave for 2 - 3 minutes, uncovered on **HIGH** until the fish is white and opaque. If using the frying pan, fry for 3 - 4 minutes on each side.

5. Squeeze lime over the fillets. Serve with rice or potatoes and a vegetable.

Serves 4. For 2 servings, halve ingredients. Preheat browning tray for 2 minutes less than the maximum recommended time.

BEEFY LASAGNE

One of my mother-in-law's recipes, this has become an all-time favorite with her family. No need to precook the noodles.

2 lbs.	ground, lean beef	1	kg
½ cup	chopped onion	125	mL
1 tsp.	garlic salt	5	mL
10 oz.	can tomato soup	284	mL
½ cup	water	125	mL
11 oz.	tomato paste	312	mL
½ cup	brewed coffee	125	mL
1 tsp.	salt	5	mL
¼ tsp.	pepper	1	mL
½ cup	sliced, fresh mushrooms	125	mL
¼ tsp.	oregano	1	mL
1 lb.	mozzarella cheese, grated	500	g
½ cup	grated Parmesan cheese	125	mL
2 cups	creamed cottage cheese	500	mL
1	egg	1	
10	uncooked lasagne noodles	10	

1. Microwave meat and onion in a microwave colander, or in a deep bowl for 5 - 6 minutes on **HIGH**. Stir frequently to break up pieces. Meat should no longer be pink, and onions should be tender and transparent.

2. Drain meat well if not using a colander. Add garlic salt, soup, water, paste, coffee, salt, pepper, mushrooms, and oregano to the meat. Cover, microwave on **HIGH** for 7 - 10 minutes, stir frequently.

3. Grease a 3-quart (3 L) casserole. Spread ⅓ of the sauce in the bottom of the greased casserole. Top with 4 or 5 noodles, broken if necessary to fit the casserole dish. Top with half of the grated cheese.

4. Mix cottage cheese with 1 egg. Spread half of this mixture over the grated mozzarella cheese. Spread with ⅓ of the meat sauce. Repeat layers, ending with the final ⅓ of the meat sauce.

5. Sprinkle the top with Parmesan cheese if desired. Cover. Microwave on **HIGH** for 8 minutes. Microwave on **MEDIUM LOW** for an additional 30 minutes or until the noodles are tender. Uncover during the last 5 minutes of cooking.

6. Let stand 10 minutes before serving.

Serves 8. Lasagne may be prepared in 2 smaller casseroles (1½ quart [1.5 L]) and half may be frozen after cooking. Defrost frozen lasagne completely before reheating. Once completely defrosted, microwave the half lasagne for 10 minutes on MEDIUM.

HOT AND SPICY CHILI

The microwave is a quick method to make this popular dish. Be sure to drain the hamburger, after it has been cooked in the microwave, as the microwaving process extracts more fat from the meat. If not drained, the chili will be greasy.

1	lb.	ground beef	500	g
1		medium onion, finely chopped	1	
1		green pepper, seeded, finely chopped	1	
1		clove garlic, minced	1	
2	tbsp.	chili powder	30	mL
½	tsp.	crushed red pepper	2	mL
1½	tsp.	salt	7	mL
1	tsp.	pepper	5	mL
5½	oz.	tomato paste	156	mL
16	oz.	canned tomatoes, undrained	500	g
16	oz.	canned kidney beans, drained	500	g
1	cup	frozen niblet corn	250	mL

1. Place beef, onion, green pepper and garlic in a large bowl. Microwave on **HIGH** for 5 - 6 minutes or until the beef is browned and the vegetables are tender. Stir frequently to break up the pieces.

2. Drain well. Add remaining ingredients. Microwave, covered to prevent splattering, for 10 - 20 minutes on **MEDIUM**. The longer the chili is microwaved, the better it will be. Stir occasionally. Serve with an assortment of toppings. These could include crisp crackers, corn chips, grated Cheddar cheese and tomato wedges.

*Serves 4. Recipe may be halved. Halve all ingredients. After adding the remaining ingredients, microwave for 10 - 20 minutes on **LOW**.*

BACON CORN BREAD

This recipe is excellent with chili or stew.

12		slices bacon	12	
1	cup	all-purpose flour	250	mL
1	cup	cornmeal	250	mL
4	tsp.	baking powder	20	mL
2	tbsp.	white granulated sugar	30	mL
½	tsp.	salt	2	mL
1		egg	1	
1	cup	milk	250	mL
2	tbsp.	butter, melted	30	mL

1. Place bacon on a roasting rack or a large plate. Cover with paper towel. Microwave on **HIGH** for 8 minutes. The bacon will be partially cooked, not crisp.

2. Place flour, cornmeal, baking powder, sugar and salt in a bowl and toss to mix. Beat egg. Add to the flour mixture.

3. Place milk in a 2-cup (500 mL) measure. Microwave on **HIGH** for 2 minutes or until small bubbles appear around the rim of the measuring cup. Add to the cornmeal mixture along with the melted butter.

4. Line the bottom of a very lightly greased 9-inch (23 cm) baking dish with waxed paper. Arrange bacon on waxed paper and along sides of pan. Pour batter carefully into the bacon-lined pan. Cover.

5. Microwave on **MEDIUM HIGH** for 4 - 5 minutes or until the cornbread appears set and a toothpick inserted into the centre comes out clean. Uncover and cool slightly.

6. Turn bread out of the pan upside-down on a board - the bacon will be on top. Remove waxed paper and cut bread into squares. Serve warm.

Serves 4 - 6. Do not halve. Keeps well in the refrigerator and is even better the next day.

APPLE-STUFFED ACORN SQUASH

There is nothing quite like the flavor of acorn squash cooked in the microwave. Nutmeg is a surprisingly complementary spice.

1	medium acorn squash	1
2 tbsp.	butter or margarine	30 mL
2 tbsp.	packed brown sugar	30 mL
1	apple peeled, cored, finely-diced	1
¼ tsp.	nutmeg	1 mL

1. Puncture the squash several times with a fork. Microwave on **HIGH** for 5 minutes. Remove from the microwave and cut in half, lengthwise.

2. Scoop out the seeds. Place 1 tbsp. (15 mL) each, of butter and brown sugar in each half. Place the apple in a 1-cup measure. Microwave on **HIGH** for 2 minutes. Spoon the apple evenly between the 2 halves.

3. Sprinkle with nutmeg. Place on a plate, cover with waxed paper, microwave on **HIGH** for 2 - 3 minutes, until squash is fork tender.

4. Let stand 2 - 3 minutes before serving.

Serves 4. May not be halved.

STUFFED POTATOES

4	large baking potatoes	4	
3 tbsp.	butter or margarine	45	mL
⅓ lb.	fresh mushrooms, chopped	150	g
⅓ cup	half-and-half	75	mL
½ tsp.	onion powder	2	mL
1 tsp.	salt	5	mL
dash	black pepper	dash	
⅓ cup	shredded sharp Cheddar cheese	75	mL

1. Scrub potatoes. Puncture each with a fork several times. Microwave for 15 - 18 minutes or until they are softened yet firm in the center. Remove from microwave, wrap in a tea towel. Let stand 5 minutes.

2. Place 1 tbsp. (15 mL) of butter in a small bowl add mushrooms. Microwave on **HIGH**, 2 - 3 minutes, until mushrooms are soft.

3. Cut a slice off the top of each potato. Carefully scoop out pulp into a bowl, reserving a thin layer inside shells. Mash pulp with remaining butter. Add half-and-half, onion powder, salt and pepper to taste. Beat until fluffy. Stir in mushrooms. Heap mixture into potato shells.

4. Arrange halves on a large plate. Sprinkle with cheese. Microwave on **HIGH** for 3 - 5 minutes, until cheese is bubbly and potato is hot.

Serves 4 - 6. To halve recipe, halve all ingredients and times.

MARINATED VEGETABLE SALAD

Best if broccoli, cauliflower, and carrots are partially cooked.

1	large head cauliflower	1	
1	large bunch broccoli	1	
5	large carrots	5	
3	stalks celery	3	
20	cherry tomatoes	20	
10 oz.	canned button mushrooms	284	mL
10 oz.	canned pitted black olives	285	mL
8 oz.	Italian or Creamy Italian Dressing	250	mL

1. Cut broccoli and cauliflower into bite-sized pieces. Peel and coin carrots. Chop celery into 1-inch pieces. Place these vegetables in a 2-quart (2 L) casserole. Cover. Microwave on **HIGH** for 6 - 7 minutes or until the vegetables are a vivid color, and just slightly softened. Cool completely.

2. Place whole cherry tomatoes, drained mushrooms, olives, and vegetables in a sealable plastic bowl. Add dressing. Seal and shake well. Marinate for 24 hours. Drain thoroughly before serving.

Serves 6 - 8. Recipe may be halved. Halve all ingredients and cooking times. It is necessary to marinate for 24 hours.

RUM CREAM PIE

This pie is a favorite of my father's and I couldn't think of a more fitting dessert for this day.

9- inch	cooked pie shell, pastry, graham wafer or chocolate wafer	23 cm	
2 tbsp.	butter	30 mL	
2 tbsp.	all-purpose flour	30 mL	
2 tbsp.	cornstarch	30 mL	
¼ cup	packed brown sugar	50 mL	
1 cup	milk	250 mL	
1 cup	half-and-half	250 mL	
3	eggs, separated	3	
⅓ cup	white rum	75 mL	
1 tbsp.	orange peel, optional	15 mL	
¾ cup	whipping cream, whipped, for garnish	175 mL	
5	fresh strawberries for garnish	5	

1. Place butter in a 1-quart (1 L) bowl. Microwave on **HIGH** for 1 minute or until melted. Stir in flour, cornstarch and brown sugar.

2. Slowly stir in milk and cream. Microwave on **HIGH** for 2 - 3 minutes or until the mixture comes to a boil. Stir every 30 seconds.

3. Add some of the hot liquid to the egg yolks. Mix well and stir the egg yolk mixture back into the hot liquid. Microwave on **HIGH** for 1 - 2 minutes or until the mixture returns to a boil. Cool slightly. Stir in rum and orange peel if using.

4. Beat egg whites until stiff peaks form. Carefully fold into rum mixture. Pour into the cooled pie shell.

5. Just prior to serving, top with whipped cream and strawberries. If whipping your own cream, use 1 tsp. (5 mL) of rum for flavoring instead of vanilla.

Serves 6. Do Not Halve.

Warm store-bought cookies to bring out a home-baked flavor. Place 2 or 3 cookies on a napkin and microwave on HIGH for 10 15 seconds.

BARBECUE

Unless you've had the luxury of a gas barbecue outside your back door all winter, July and August will be prime barbecueing time. The microwave oven can be a useful sidekick to the barbecue.

Don't be afraid to barbecue extras when the grill is hot. If the meat is well cooked it will freeze safely and well. On one of those rushed evenings, the meat can be defrosted and reheated in the microwave, retaining all the original barbecued flavor. When reheating meat, try covering it with a piece of lettuce instead of microwave-safe plastic wrap or waxed paper. The lettuce imparts a delicate flavor and helps keep the meat moist.

No matter what method you use to cook chicken, it should be well done. It's difficult to completely cook chicken on hot coals without burning the skin, and even harder when you brush it with a barbecue sauce. To alleviate this problem, precook the completely defrosted chicken in the microwave, for 6 minutes per pound (13 minutes/kg) on **HIGH**. It will still be slightly pink. From this stage of doneness it's much easier to finish cooking on the barbecue without burning. Chicken is excellent if marinated in Teriyaki sauce for 5 - 6 hours before cooking.

For barbecued roast beef the order of microwaving/barbecuing is reversed from chicken. It is difficult to judge the doneness of a barbecued roast because the temperature at which the roast is cooking is so hard to determine. Barbecue your roast, with the sauces or spices you would normally use, until it is suitably charbrowned. Remove it from the grill, place it on a roasting rack or an inverted saucer in a pie dish, and insert your probe or microwave thermometer. You will need either a probe or a microwave meat thermometer to accurately finish cooking the roast. The auto-cook or sensor systems will not work with a partially cooked roast. Once you've inserted the probe, program the oven to the desired doneness (for example, a medium-done roast requires a setting of 150oF (67°F)) Microwave on **MEDIUM** until it reaches the desired doneness. To help keep your oven clean, cover the roast loosely with waxed paper.

BARBECUE (cont'd.)

If you don't like waiting 45 minutes for potatoes to cook on the coals, precook them in the microwave. Cook each medium potato for 3 minutes on HIGH. The potatoes should be washed and punctured several times with a fork before microwaving, but they don't need to be wrapped and can be put right on the oven floor. After partially cooking, slit the potatoes lengthwise, dab with butter, add a few lightly sautéed green peppers and mushrooms and wrap tightly with foil. The potatoes can then be placed on the grill and will require about 10 minutes of barbecuing, depending on their size and the heat of the coals. Test for doneness with a fork.

Corn on the cob is delicious when microwaved, but even better if it has a few minutes on the coals afterward. Presoak the corn on the cob, right in the husk, in a sinkful of cold water for 15 minutes before microwaving. Shake excess water off the corn and microwave on HIGH for 3 minutes per husk. Microwave a maximum of 6 ears at a time. Place the microwaved husks over very hot coals for 4 - 5 minutes. They'll scorch somewhat, but don't worry the blacker the husks, the better the flavor inside. The real trick lies in trying to get the corn out of the husks while it's still piping hot. You have to be very quick!

Ribs are super on the barbecue, but if improperly cooked they can be tough. It helps to precook them in the microwave, then barbecue to brown them, and impart that grilled flavor. To precook, place the ribs in a casserole and cover with water. For every 1 lb. of ribs, add ¼ cup (50 mL) of vinegar to the water. The vinegar tenderizes and helps extract fat. Microwave, covered, on HIGH for 5 minutes and then on MEDIUM for at least 7 - 10 minutes / lb. (16 - 20 minutes/ Kg) The longer you simmer them, the more tender they'll be. Stir frequently. Drain the water and place the ribs - brushed with your favorite sauce - on the barbecue.

If either ends of fish fillets are thinner than the middle, fold the thin ends under. Doubling up of the fish at the ends helps to prevent over-cooking at these parts.

SWEET AND SOUR SAUCE

This sauce is excellent with poultry, pork or fish. Remember to partially cook the meat in the microwave before adding the sauce. Because of the high sugar content of the sauce, it will burn easily on the barbecue.

1¾ cup	water or chicken broth	525 mL
1 cup	packed brown sugar	250 mL
1 cup	cider vinegar	250 mL
1	lemon, juice of	1
2	green onions, chopped	2
1	clove garlic, crushed	1
¼ cup	ketchup	50 mL
2 tbsp.	dry sherry	30 mL
2 tbsp.	soy sauce	30 mL
2 tbsp.	cornstarch	30 mL

1. Combine all ingredients in a medium-sized bowl. Stir to blend well.

2. Microwave on **HIGH** for 3 - 5 minutes or until the mixture clears and thickens. Stir 3 - 4 times during microwaving.

Makes 3½ cups of sauce.

SPICY ORANGE BARBECUE SAUCE

This sauce is excellent on ham steaks, chicken, and ribs.

6 oz.	can frozen orange juice conc.	178 mL
⅔ cup	water	150 mL
2 tbsp.	soy sauce	30 mL
1 tbsp.	prepared mustard	15 mL
½ tsp.	Tabasco sauce	2 mL
¼ cup	packed brown sugar	50 mL
½ cup	vegetable oil	125 mL

1. Combine all ingredients in a small bowl.

2. Microwave on **HIGH** for 2 - 3 minutes. Watch carefully as mixture may boil over. If it seems to be boiling too vigorously, turn your power level down to **MEDIUM**.

3. Brush on partially grilled meat. Baste with sauce as needed during the barbecueing.

Makes 2 cups of sauce.

SMOKY BARBECUE SAUCE

Serve this sauce with beef, pork, chicken or fish. The recipe makes 5 cups (1.25 L) so have a large container ready and store in the refrigerator to use when needed.

2	cloves garlic, crushed	2
½ cup	finely chopped onion	125 mL
½ cup	finely chopped green pepper	125 mL
½ cup	finely chopped celery	125 mL
½ tsp.	oregano	2 mL
½ tsp.	basil	2 mL
½ tsp.	cinnamon	2 mL
1 tsp.	salt	5 mL
1	lemon, juiced, rind	1
⅛ tsp.	Tabasco sauce	0.5 mL
1½ tbsp.	Worcestershire sauce	23 mL
1½ tbsp.	liquid smoke	23 mL
2 cups	ketchup	500 mL
1 cup	water	250 mL
½ cup	cider vinegar	125 mL

1. Microwave garlic, onion, green pepper and celery on **HIGH** for 2 - 3 minutes or until the vegetables are tender.

2. Add remaining ingredients, cover, and microwave on **LOW** for 30 minutes, stirring occasionally. Cool.

3. Baste meats with sauce while barbecuing.

Makes 5 cups of sauce. May be halved. Do NOT halve simmering time.

Homemade croutons add a special touch to green salads. 3 cups (750 mL) of bread cubes, lightly coated with ¼ cup (50 mL) melted butter will dry to crispness when arranged on double thick paper towels and microwaved on HIGH 2 - 3 minutes. Stir or toss every minute to prevent burning. For seasoned croutons, add ½ tsp. dried parsley flakes, oregano or Italian seasoning to melted butter. Other seasonings to add: ¼ tsp. (1 mL) garlic salt, seasoned salt or chili powder. Whole-wheat, rye or pumpernickel breads also make delicious croutons.

MAPLE-BARBECUED SPARERIBS

Serve with white rice, tossed salad and lots of napkins.

3 lbs.	pork, side spareribs	1.5	kg
	water to cover		
¾ cup	vinegar	175	mL
1 cup	maple syrup	250	mL
1 tbsp.	chili sauce	15	mL
1 tbsp.	vinegar (second amount)	15	mL
1 tbsp.	Worcestershire sauce	15	mL
1	small onion, finely chopped	1	
½ tsp.	salt	2	mL
¼ tsp.	dry mustard	1	mL
⅛ tsp.	freshly ground pepper	0.5	mL

1. Cut ribs into serving-sized pieces; place in a 3-quart (3 L) casserole. Cover with water. Add vinegar, and cover the casserole. Microwave on **HIGH** for 5 minutes. Reduce the power level and continue microwaving for an additional 30 minutes on **MEDIUM**. Stir occasionally. Drain.

2. Combine remaining ingredients in a medium-sized bowl and microwave for 5 - 6 minutes. The sauce should boil for 5 minutes.

3. Place ribs on a high rack over coals. Baste with sauce. Barbecue until the ribs are dark brown. Brush with sauce frequently. Serve any extra sauce on the side.

Serves 6. May be halved. Halve ingredients. Simmer the ribs for the same amount of time. Boil the sauce for 5 complete minutes.

See photograph page 64A.

BAKED BEANS

There seems to be no more fitting accompaniment to a barbecue than a tasty, wholesome bowl of baked beans. This recipe is from my mother-in-law, Jenny Dams.

2 cups	dried white beans	500	mL
½ tsp.	baking soda	2	mL
4 tbsp.	packed brown sugar	60	mL
2 tbsp.	molasses	30	mL
1 tbsp.	dried mustard	15	mL
	salt and pepper to taste		
1	small onion, chopped	1	
8	slices slightly cooked bacon or ham or side pork	8	
½ cup	ketchup	125	mL

BAKED BEANS (cont'd.)

1. Soak beans in a 3-quart (3 L) casserole overnight in water to cover. Drain. Cover beans with fresh water, add soda, cover and microwave on **HIGH** for 40 minutes. Stir 2 or 3 times. Drain.

2. Mix remaining ingredients together. Pour over the slightly softened beans and microwave on **MEDIUM** for 45 minutes - 1½ hours, or until the beans are completely softened. Add more water if necessary. Cover while microwaving. Cool slightly. Serve.

Serves 6. Do not halve recipe.

See photograph page 64A.

BROCCOLI, ASPARAGUS OR GREEN BEANS WITH SESAME-SOY TOPPING

Any of these vegetables is suitable with this very simple topping.

1 lb.	fresh broccoli, asparagus or green beans	500 g
2 tsp.	sesame oil	10 mL
2 tbsp.	soy sauce	30 mL
1 tbsp.	sesame seeds	15 mL

1. Trim vegetables. Cut into serving-sized pieces. Place in a medium-sized casserole dish. Cover and microwave on **HIGH** for 4 - 7 minutes or until fork tender. Do NOT overcook.

2. Drain off any extra water. Sprinkle with remaining ingredients. Toss to coat evenly. Serve immediately.

Serves 4 - 6. Recipe may be halved. Halve ingredients and cooking times.

See photograph page 48A.

To speed up the preparation of frozen hash browns, microwave on HIGH until thawed, and then brown in a frying pan or browning dish.

SEASONED FRENCH BREAD

Fresh warm buttered bread goes well with any barbecue meal. This is particularly tasty because of the addition of herbs and spices.

1 loaf	French Bread	1	
½ cup	butter, softened	125	mL
1 tsp.	dried parsley flakes	5	mL
½ tsp.	thyme	2	mL
½ tsp.	oregano	2	mL
½ tsp.	rosemary	2	mL
¼ cup	Parmesan cheese	50	mL

1. Cut the bread into slices.

2. Mix the remaining ingredients together. Spread on the sliced bread.

3. Wrap the loaf with a tea towel, and place in a wicker basket. Microwave on **HIGH** for 1 - 1½ minutes or until the bread JUST feels warm.

Serves 6.

See photograph page 64A.

PEACH AND RASPBERRY LAYERED CHEESECAKE

This cheesecake is simple to make, requires no baking, yet looks like you have lavished a great deal of time on it.

CRUST:

¾ cup	graham wafer crumbs	175	mL
⅓ cup	ground almonds	75	mL
¼ cup	packed brown sugar	50	mL
⅓ cup	butter or margarine	75	mL

PEACH LAYER:

4	large peaches	4	
2 tbsp.	gelatin (2 envelopes)	30	mL
2 cups	cream cheese	500	g
1 cup	white granulated sugar	250	mL
1 cup	whipping cream	250	mL
1 tsp.	vanilla	5	mL

RASPBERRY LAYER:

2 cups	fresh raspberries or 14 oz. (425 g) frozen, thawed, drained	500	mL
2 tsp.	honey	10	mL
2 tbsp.	gelatin (2 envelopes)	30	mL
¼ cup	orange brandy	50	mL

PEACH AND RASPBERRY LAYERED CHEESECAKE (cont'd.)

1. In a small bowl, combine wafer crumbs, almonds, brown sugar and butter. Mix very well. Press into the bottom of a straight-sided 9-inch (23 cm) circular dish. (You could also use a 10-inch (25 cm) springform pan and bake the crust in a preheated 375°F (190°C) oven for 10 minutes, if you prefer.) Microwave on **HIGH** for 1½ - 2 minutes. Cool.

2. Place 2 peaches on the floor of the microwave, and microwave on **HIGH** for 2 minutes or until the peaches are just beginning to feel warm to touch. Let stand 2 minutes. Repeat with remaining 2 peaches. Cool. The peaches will now peel more easily. Peel and chop peaches, discarding pits and skin. In a food processor or blender, process peaches until puréed.

3. Spoon ½ cup (125 mL) puréed peaches in a small bowl. Sprinkle with gelatin. Mix very well. Microwave on **HIGH** for 1 - 2 minutes, or until the gelatin is dissolved. Watch carefully so that the fruit does not boil over.

4. In a mixing bowl, beat cream cheese until softened. Add sugar, whipping cream and vanilla; beat until creamy and thickened. Fold peach mixtures, both the one with gelatin and the one without, into the cheese mixture until blended. Set aside.

5. Rinse fresh raspberries under cold running water. In processor or blender, combine raspberries and honey; process until puréed. Strain through sieve into small bowl to remove seeds.

6. Spoon ¼ cup (50 mL) of the strained mixture into a small dish. Sprinkle with gelatin. Microwave on **HIGH** for 1 - 2 minutes or until the gelatin is dissolved. Watch carefully so that the fruit does not boil over. Add liqueur.

7. Assemble. Reserve ½ cup (125 mL) of the raspberry filling for garnish. Spread half of the remaining raspberry filling evenly over the crust. Freeze for 8 - 10 minutes or until set. Spoon half of the peach filling over raspberry layer. Freeze for 12 minutes or until firm. Repeat with remaining raspberry filling and remaining peach filling.

8. Spoon reserved raspberry filling onto the top of the cheesecake. Swirl with a knife to completely cover. May be served with a dollop of whipped cream.

Serves 6.

Before adding flavored gelatin, heat water to boiling in a bowl suitable for a microwave oven, or dissolve unflavored gelatin in a measuring cup filled with the appropriate amount of fluid or liquid, then heat in the microwave oven. Cleaning a measuring cup is much easier than cleaning a saucepan.

GRAND MARNIER CHOCOLATE MOCHA ICE CREAM

You don't need an ice cream maker to make this delicious creamy ice cream.

6	egg yolks	6
1 cup	white granulated sugar	250 mL
½ tsp.	salt	2 mL
4 cups	whipping cream (divided)	1 L
8 oz.	semisweet chocolate	250 g
½ cup	brewed mocha java coffee	125 mL
2 tbsp.	ground mocha java coffee beans	30 mL
⅓ cup	Grand Marnier (optional)	75 mL

1. Beat together egg yolks, sugar and salt until the mixture is thick and pale yellow in color. When dropped from a spoon the mixture should form a thick ribbon and not separate into smaller drips.

2. Beat in 2 cups whipping cream. Microwave on **MEDIUM** for 5 - 8 minutes until the mixture thickens enough to lightly coat a spoon. Stir frequently.

3. Set aside custard mixture to cool. Meanwhile, place chocolate and brewed mocha coffee in a medium-sized bowl Microwave on **MEDIUM HIGH** for 3 - 5 minutes or until the chocolate is completely melted. Stir frequently. Cool slightly.

4. Add ground coffee beans. The ground coffee beans are surprisingly different and delicious in this ice cream; however, they may not be well accepted by children. Chocolate-covered almonds, raisins or peanuts are an excellent substitute.

5. Stir the custard into the chocolate mixture. Chill for 5 minutes. Whip the remaining whipping cream until firm. Fold in the Grand Marnier and the chilled custard mixture.

6. If you have an ice cream maker then chill the above mixture in the ice cream maker until it is set. If you do not have an ice cream maker then place the mixture, covered, in a freezer for 2 hours. Remove and beat the mixture well. Cover with plastic wrap and return it to the freezer for 3 - 4 hours or until it is completely frozen.

Makes 1 quart (1 L). Do not halve. Ice cream keeps well in the freezer.

Remove freezer paper easily from frozen packages after heating 15 seconds on HIGH. Let stand 2 - 3 minutes before peeling off loosened paper.

JULY 1ST: SUMMER BARBECUE

Clockwise From Foreground
1. Maple-Barbecued Spareribs, page 60
2. Corn On The Cob, page 72
3. Seasoned French Bread, page 62
4. Peanut Parfait, page 65
5. Baked Beans, page 60

PEANUT PARFAIT

A quick and easy dessert that looks attractive and can be made ahead of time.

¾ cup	quick-cooking rolled oats	175 mL
⅓ cup	packed brown sugar	75 mL
¼ cup	chopped peanuts	50 mL
3 tbsp.	butter, melted	45 mL
½ cup	packed brown sugar	125 mL
¼ cup	all-purpose flour	50 mL
2 cups	milk	500 mL
2	egg yolks, beaten	2
⅔ cup	creamy peanut butter	150 mL
½ tsp.	vanilla	2 mL

1. Stir together oats, the ⅓ cup (75 mL) brown sugar, peanuts and butter.

2. Spread the mixture in the bottom of a large, flat casserole dish. Microwave on **HIGH**, uncovered, for 2 - 4 minutes, stirring occasionally. Mixture should be dry and crumbly. Be careful not to overcook, however, as mixture scorches easily. Cool and crumble.

3. Combine brown sugar and flour in a medium-sized bowl. Blend in milk and egg yolks. Microwave, uncovered, on **HIGH** for 3 - 5 minutes or until the mixture is bubbly. Microwave on **HIGH** for an additional minute.

4. Stir in peanut butter and vanilla. Cover surface with waxed paper to prevent skin from forming. Chill.

5. Alternate layers of pudding and oatmeal in parfait glasses. Garnish with whipped cream and a strawberry.

Serves 5 - 6. Recipe may be halved. Halve all ingredients and microwave times.

See photograph page 64A.

Egg yolks are higher in fat content and absorb more microwave energy than the white of the egg. To avoid the yolk cooking before the white does, microwave eggs on LOW. Each egg will require 1 - 1½ minutes of microwaving time on LOW. If you do not have a low setting use POWER LEVEL 3. Cover while microwaving.

GARDEN HARVEST

There is nothing like the flavor of vegetables just after they are picked. The microwave oven enhances the flavor of vegetables, so that they do not lose any of that un-matched just-picked flavor. Many of us are faced with the dilemma of what to do with bumper crops. Pickling, canning, blanching and an abundance of delicious recipes all help put a dent in the bushels of vegetables we, in this country, have the good fortune of reaping. With the help of your microwave, putting up this years crop will be the most enjoyable and delicious that it's ever been.

PICKLED BEETS

These may be served hot or cold.

5	medium beets	5
¼ cup	chopped onion	50 mL
1 tbsp.	butter or margarine	15 mL
1 tsp.	white granulated sugar	5 mL
2 tbsp.	white vinegar	30 mL
¼ tsp.	black pepper	1 mL
¼ tsp.	salt	1 mL
¼ cup	chopped green pepper	50 mL

1. Remove the leaves from the beets, leaving about 1 inch (3 cm) of stalk on top of the beet. Place beets in a 1-quart (1 L) bowl. Add ½ cup (125 mL) water to the beets. Cover.

2. Microwave on **HIGH** for 10 - 12 minutes or until the beets are fork tender. Cool slightly. Run under cold water and rub gently to remove skin.

3. Slice beets. Microwave onion and butter in a 2-quart (2 L) casserole for 3 minutes on **HIGH** or until the onions are tender and transparent.

4. Add sugar, vinegar, black pepper, salt, green pepper and beets. Cover. Microwave on **HIGH** for 4 minutes. Stir once.

Serves 4. Recipe may be halved. Halve all ingredients and microwaving times.

VEGETABLE BOUQUET

There is nothing like the flavor of fresh-picked vegetables. All that is needed is a pat of butter and salt and pepper to taste.

¼ lb.	green or yellow beans, trimmed	115 g
¼ lb.	baby carrots, scraped	115 g
¼ lb.	green peas, shelled	115 g
8	tiny white onions	8
2 - 3 tbsp.	butter	30 - 45 mL
	salt and pepper to taste	

1. Place all vegetables together in a medium-sized casserole. Sprinkle with 1 tbsp. (15 mL) of water. Cover. Microwave on **HIGH** for 6 - 8 minutes or until bright and vivid in color and tender-crisp.

2. Drain. Toss with butter and salt and pepper.

Serves 6. To halve recipe, halve all ingredients and times.

ZUCCHINI-STUFFED TOMATOES

A great combination of 2 garden specialties, tomatoes and zucchini.

4	medium tomatoes	4
¼ cup	butter or margarine	50 mL
2	medium zucchini, diced	2
1	medium onion, finely chopped	1
1 tsp.	garlic powder	5 mL
¼ tsp.	basil leaves	1 mL
⅛ tsp.	black pepper	0.5 mL
½ lb.	fresh mushrooms, sliced	250 g
1 cup	croutons	250 mL

1. Cut a thin slice from the top of each tomato; scoop out pulp, reserve, leaving a thin shell. Chop pulp finely.

2. Combine butter, zucchini, onion, garlic, basil, pepper and tomato pulp in a medium-sized bowl. Cover. Microwave on **HIGH** for 4 - 5 minutes or until the vegetables are just beginning to soften.

3. Add mushrooms, cover, continue microwaving on **HIGH** 2 - 3 more minutes, until zucchini is tender but not mushy. Stir in croutons.

4. Spoon mixture immediately into tomato shells. Place tomatoes in baking dish, and just before serving microwave on **HIGH** for 1 - 2 minutes or until hot. Do not overcook.

Serves 4. Recipe may be halved or doubled. Adjust times correspondingly by halving or doubling microwaving times.

ZUCCHINI WITH MUSHROOMS AND TOMATOES

This is a delicious casserole, and takes just under 15 minutes to prepare.

2 tbsp.	butter or margarine	30	mL
2 tsp.	fresh parsley	10	mL
2 tbsp.	chopped onion	30	mL
½ lb.	fresh mushrooms, chopped	250	g
3	medium zucchini, thinly sliced	3	
1	tomato, peeled and diced	1	
1 tsp.	salt	5	mL
¼ tsp.	cayenne	1	mL
¼ tsp.	garlic powder	1	mL
½ cup	Cheddar cheese, grated	125	mL
½ cup	dry bread crumbs	125	mL

1. Microwave butter, parsley, onion and mushrooms for 2 minutes on **HIGH**, in a 3-quart (3 L) casserole or until the onions are tender and transparent and the mushrooms are softened.

2. Add zucchini, tomato and seasonings. Cover. Microwave on **HIGH** for 4 - 6 minutes or until the zucchini is just beginning to soften.

3. Stir in cheese. Top with bread crumbs. Microwave on **HIGH** for an additional 3 - 5 minutes or until the cheese is melted and the zucchini is tender.

Serves 6. Recipe may be halved. Halve all ingredients and cooking times.

Hasten the ripening of an avocado by microwaving it on MEDIUM for 2 minutes. Turn avocado over and microwave on MEDIUM for 1 minute longer.

Freeze left-over rice for up to a month. To defrost and heat to serving temperature, microwave on HIGH for 2 - 3 minutes for 1 serving, or, 4 - 6 minutes for 2 servings.

BULGAR-STUFFED SQUASH

A unique way to serve squash.

½	large squash such as hubbard, butternut, spaghetti or turban	½
1 tsp.	butter or margarine	5 mL
1	clove garlic, minced	1
½ cup	chopped walnuts or pecans	125 mL
2 cups	cooked bulgar or rice	500 mL
2	green onions, chopped	2
1	large tomato, chopped	1
¼ cup	chicken broth	50 mL
½ tsp.	rosemary	2 mL
½ tsp.	oregano	2 mL
½ tsp.	basil	2 mL
	salt and pepper to taste	
¾ cup	shredded Swiss, Monterey Jack or mozzarella cheese	175 mL

1. Place squash, cut-side down, on the bottom of a platter or pie plate. Sprinkle 2 tsp. (10 mL) of water on the bottom. Cover with microwave-safe plastic wrap. Microwave on **HIGH** for 5 - 9 minutes or until the squash is just fork-tender.

2. Scoop out the cooked squash flesh, leaving about a ½-inch (1.25 cm) shell. Chop squash, or separate into strands if using spaghetti squash. Set aside.

3. Microwave butter, garlic and walnuts in a large microwave safe bowl for 2 minutes on **HIGH**. Stir in cooked bulgar or rice, green onions, tomato, and broth or water. Microwave on **HIGH** for 3 - 5 minutes or until piping hot.

4. Blend in herbs, salt and pepper as desired, and squash pieces. Spoon filling into shells. Place in a pie plate or on a platter. Cover with a microwave-safe plastic wrap. Microwave on **HIGH** for 5 minutes. Remove wrap. Sprinkle with cheese.

5. Microwave an additional 1 - 3 minutes or until the cheese is melted and the filling piping-hot.

Serves 4. Do not Halve.

Rice should be washed before being microwaved to remove extra starch. Once washed, microwaved rice cooks up light and fluffy.

GARDEN RELISH

If you layer the vegetables in a large jar, they look very attractive.
Keeps for 1 - 2 weeks in the refrigerator.

½ lb.	baby carrots, scraped	250	g
1	cucumber	1	
2	stalks celery	2	
2	green or red peppers	2	
1	small cauliflower	1	
¼ lb.	green beans, trimmed	125	g
12	small white onions, peeled	12	
¼ cup	salt	50	mL
3 cups	white vinegar	750	mL
3 cups	water	750	mL
1½ cups	white granulated sugar	375	mL
¼ cup	mustard seed	50	mL
1 tsp.	dried tarragon	5	mL
¾ tsp.	celery seed	4	mL
¾ tsp.	mace	4	mL
½ lb.	mushrooms, vertically sliced	250	g

1. Slice carrots, cucumber and celery. Cut peppers into strips or rings. Break cauliflower into florets. Combine all with beans and onions in a bowl and sprinkle with salt. Cover and set aside for 2 hours.

2. Rinse vegetables and dry well. Combine vinegar, water, sugar and seasonings in a large microwave-safe bowl. Microwave on **HIGH** for 6 - 7 minutes or until mixture comes to a boil. Boil for 2 minutes.

3. Add rinsed vegetables and mushrooms. Cover. Microwave on **HIGH** until the mixture returns to a boil. Remove from the microwave and cool. Chill several hours. Cover. Keeps 1 - 2 weeks.

Makes 2½ quarts (2.5 L). Recipe can be halved.

Microwave cooking setting and times should serve as a guide and are usually based on ovens of 700 watts. As a rule of thumb, HIGH indicates 100 percent, MEDIUM HIGH indicates 70 percent, MEDIUM 50 percent and LOW 30 percent. However, keep in mind that some ovens operate on lower wattage. In addition, other factors such as the amount of food cooked at one time and the density of the food affect both the power level and length of time required to cook foods.

ELEGANT GREEN BEANS

Adapted to the microwave from a conventional recipe in "Gardening Under the Arch" by the Millarville (Alberta, Canada) Horticultural Society, this terrific recipe is great year-round. If fresh beans aren't available, frozen will suffice.

4 cups	trimmed green beans	1	kg
¼ cup	chopped onion	50	mL
3 tbsp.	butter or margarine	45	mL
2 tbsp.	all-purpose flour	30	mL
2 tbsp.	sugar	30	mL
2 tbsp.	white vinegar	30	mL
¼ cup	snipped, fresh parsley	50	mL
1 cup	sour cream	250	mL
3	slices bacon, cooked crisp	3	

1. Place green beans in a medium-sized bowl. Sprinkle with water until they are approximately half-covered. Cover the dish. Microwave on **HIGH** for 6 - 9 minutes or until the beans are tender and bright green in color. Drain. Reserve liquid. Add enough water to drained liquid to make 1 cup (250 mL).

2. Microwave onion and butter in a 2-quart (2 L) casserole for 2 - 3 minutes or until the onion is tender and transparent. Stir in bean liquid, flour, sugar, vinegar and parsley. Microwave on **HIGH** for 2 - 3 minutes or until the mixture is thickened, stirring every minute.

3. Add sour cream and fold in the beans. Crumble bacon over the top. Microwave on **HIGH** for 2 - 4 minutes until heated, but not boiling.

Serves 6 - 8 persons. The recipe may be halved. Halve all ingredients and cooking times.

Make a brown butter sauce for fresh, cooked vegetables by microwaving ½ cup (125 mL) butter in waxed paper-covered bowl on HIGH for 5 - 6 minutes or until golden brown, stirring every 2 minutes.

CARROTS WITH HONEY

Sweet, garden-fresh carrots only require minimal amounts of water added to them before microwaving. If the carrots are older and drier it is necessary to completely cover them with water or stock before microwaving.

1 lb.	carrots	500 g
1 cup	water (if necessary)	250 mL
	salt to taste	
2½ tbsp.	honey	40 mL
1 tbsp.	butter	15 mL

1. Peel and slice carrots into evenly sized coins. Place in a 1-quart (1 L) casserole and add water if necessary. Microwave on **HIGH** for 5 - 8 minutes or until the carrots are tender. Drain.

2. Season to taste with salt. Stir in honey and butter until both are melted and the carrots are thoroughly coated.

Serves 4.

MICROWAVE TIMINGS FOR COMMON VEGETABLES

VEGETABLE	QUANTITY	WATER	TIMING
Artichokes	1 medium	4 tbsp. (60 mL)	8 - 10 minutes
Asparagus	1 lb. (450 g)	2 tbsp. (30 mL)	9 - 12 minutes
Beans, green	1 lb. (450 g)	½ cup (125 mL)	7 - 8 minutes
Broccoli	1 lb. (450 g)	1 tbsp. (15 mL)	7 - 8 minutes
Brussels sprouts	1 lb. (450 g)	1 tbsp. (15 mL)	7 - 8 minutes
Cabbage	1 lb. (450 g)	½ cup (125 mL)	9 - 10 minutes
Carrots	8 oz. (250 g)	¼ cup (50 mL)	5 - 6 minutes
Cauliflower	8 oz. (250 g)	1 tbsp. (15 mL)	7 - 8 minutes
Corn, on cob	4 with husks	soak, shake dry	15 minutes
Mushrooms, whole	8 oz. (225 g)	none	2 - 3 minutes
Onions	2 medium, whole	none	9 - 10 minutes
Parsnips	1 lb. (450 g)	¼ cup (50 mL)	8 - 9 minutes
Peas, green	l lb. (450 g)	2 tbsp. (30 mL)	7 - 8 minutes
Potatoes	4 medium	none	15- 16 minutes
Spinach	1 lb. (450 g)	none	5 - 6 minutes
Sweet Potato	1 medium	none, leave skin on	8 - 9 minutes

BLANCHING VEGETABLES

The microwave oven is a wonderful asset for those who like to freeze vegetables when they are at their peak. Fresh supermarket produce can be blanched and frozen, and home gardeners can also make use of this ideal way to preserve the vegetable crop. Vegetables can be picked as they reach their peak flavor, even if you only have a few servings. Without the bother of heavy pots, and working in a steamy hot kitchen, you'll have vegetables blanched and ready to freeze in minutes.

Vegetables should be prepared as you would for regular cooking. Remember that blanching does not make substandard vegetables any better; always start with a high quality, unblemished product.

Using the chart opposite as a guideline, place the prepared vegetables in a 1-quart (1 L) casserole, and add the appropriate amount of water. DO NOT SALT. Cover with a lid, or a dinner plate. Microwave on **HIGH** for half of the minimum time given.

The vegetables should be an evenly bright color. If the vegetables are not evenly bright, cook at 30 second intervals, until they are.

Drain vegetables and plunge immediately into ice water to prevent further cooking. This is particularly important when blanching in the microwave because carry-over cooking is exaggerated.

Blot the vegetables on paper towel to absorb any excess moisture. Wrap them tightly in serving-sized containers, or in microwave-safe plastic wrap. If the vegetables are frozen in microwave-safe containers, they can be cooked in the same container.

Make sure the package of vegetables is tightly sealed, with all of the air removed from the inside. Label the packages with type of vegetables, amount and date.

For vegetables not given on the chart on page 72 the blanching time is ½ of the time given in most basic microwave cookbooks.

HINTS: To remove the skins from carrots easily, cover them with boiling water and let stand for a few minutes until the skin loosens. To keep cauliflower white for freezing, use half water and half milk.

Almost every microwave cookbook advises not to sprinkle the surface of meats and vegetables with salt before microwaving. Salt has 2 adverse effects:

1. Food sprinkled with table salt tends to cook unevenly in the microwave. Some foods will blacken where the salt has been sprinkled.

2. Salt also dries out the surface of foods, while they are microwaving.

Your salt intake can be greatly reduced and flavor still enhanced by the use of herb mixtures.

BLEND FOR MEAT, POTATOES AND VEGETABLES

4 tsp.	dry mustard	20 mL
2 tsp.	sage	10 mL
2 tsp.	thyme	10 mL
1 tsp.	marjoram	5 mL

1. Mix all seasonings together well. Store, labelled, in an airtight container.

Makes approximately ¼ cup.

AMERICAN HEART ASSOCIATION HERB MIX (ALL-PURPOSE)

½ tsp.	cayenne	2 mL
1 tbsp.	garlic powder	15 mL
1 tsp.	ground basil	5 mL
1 tsp.	ground thyme	5 mL
1 tsp.	parsley	5 mL
1 tsp.	savory	5 mL
1 tsp.	mace	5 mL
1 tsp.	onion powder	5 mL
1 tsp.	black pepper	5 mL
1 tsp.	sage	5 mL

NOTE: If you are using leaves, use 1½ tsp. (7 mL) of basil, parsley and sage and 1¼ tsp. (6 mL) of thyme and savory.

1. Combine all of the seasonings in a blender jar. Blend the ingredients at medium-high speed until they are ground. If you don't have a blender, shake, until very well mixed, in a plastic container.

2. Store in an airtight container.

Makes ½ cup.

DRYING FLOWERS

It is necessary to use blossoms of top quality and freshness. Some of the best drying ones include sweet peas, snap dragons, delphiniums, pansies, violets, carnations, marigolds, and lobelia. Flowers that DO NOT dry well are petunias, lilies, and geraniums.

You will need:
A microwave-safe, deep-sided dish, large enough for 2 - 3 blossoms.
Dry, dustless kitty litter
Thin wire for stems, optional
Oasis, optional. This is put in the vase in which you will be arranging the flowers, to hold them in place. It is available in any florist shop.
Shadow Frame, optional

1. Place 4 cups (1 L) of kitty litter (that's right) in the microwave dish. Make sure it is the dustless kitty litter as the other types will coat the flowers and give them a dull appearance (and attract the kitties).

2. Cut the blossoms as you are drying them. Pick only the freshest blossoms.

3. Hollow out a well in the kitty litter in which to place the blossom. Very carefully place kitty litter over the blossom. For the smaller more intricate flowers, tweezers help to position the litter in the smaller "nooks and crannies". Try to keep the shape of the flower as close as possible to its natural shape.

4. Once the flower is completely and carefully covered with litter, place the bowl in the microwave. It is best not to do any more than 2 or 3 small blossoms at a time, as some may scorch. In 1 microwaving session, it is possible to dry 1 stem of sweet peas with 3 - 4 large blossoms OR 3 pansies OR a large stem full of snapdragons.

5. Microwave the flowers on **HIGH** for 2 minutes. The kitty litter should feel hot to touch, but not hot enough that it cannot be touched. You will notice a little condensation around the sides of the dish; this is normal.

6. Let the kitty litter cool completely before removing the flowers. Remove carefully, and blow off any litter that may adhere to the blossom.

7. Once the flowers are cleaned off and ready to arrange, they may be lightly sprayed with an unscented hairspray, to help preserve them.

8. If you want to speed-up the whole process, you can have 3 or 4 containers filled with kitty litter ready to go 1 after the other. Always mark the location of the blossoms if you are doing this.

9. The litter can be reused many times. Cool before using.

BACK TO SCHOOL

September - possibly the years' busiest month. School resumes, evening activities begin, and the lazy days of summer are finished. There are nights that a frozen casserole, or a quick and easy meal is a welcome treat, if not a necessity. The microwave oven is well-suited to this type of schedule, and taste does not have to be compromised. A delicious assortment of casseroles and quick meals, complemented by tasty desserts will sooth even the most frazzled of us.

SPICED CABBAGE-SAUSAGE CASSEROLE

This quick-to-fix dish is spiced with an unusual combination of herbs and peppers. For less heat, cut down on, or eliminate, cayenne and/or black pepper. Serve with sliced tomatoes and rye bread.

1 lb.	Kielbassa or other smoked, fully cooked sausage	450 g
1 tbsp.	butter or margarine	15 mL
2	medium onions, cut julienne	2
½	medium head of cabbage, shredded	½
½ cup	chicken broth	125 mL
1	bay leaf	1
1	apple, pared, cut julienne	1
2 tbsp.	brown sugar	30 mL
1 tsp.	salt	5 mL
¾ tsp.	paprika	4 mL
½ tsp.	white pepper	2 mL
¼ tsp.	EACH: onion powder, garlic powder, cayenne pepper, black pepper, dried thyme and basil leaves	1 mL

1. Cut sausage into 3-inch (7.5 cm) lengths on the diagonal.

2. Microwave butter, onions, cabbage, chicken broth and bay leaf in a large casserole dish, covered, on **HIGH** for 5 minutes.

3. Add remaining ingredients along with the sausage. Cover and microwave on **LOW** for an additional 8 - 12 minutes or until the cabbage is tender and the sausage is piping hot. Remove bay leaf.

4. Serve portions of the cabbage topped with pieces of sausage.

Serves 4. To serve 2, halve all ingredients and cooking times.

STROGANOFF MEATBALLS

The meatballs can be made well in advance, and frozen until ready to use. Thaw the meatballs and add it to this quickly prepared sauce for a gourmet supper in a hurry.

½ lb.	lean ground beef	450 g	
1 oz.	dehydrated onion soup mix	28 g	
¼ cup	fine dry bread crumbs	50 mL	
¼ cup	evaporated milk	50 mL	
2 tbsp.	butter or margarine	30 mL	
1 cup	sliced, fresh mushrooms	250 mL	
½ cup	chopped onion	125 mL	
1	clove of garlic	1	
2 tbsp.	all-purpose flour	30 mL	
1 tbsp.	ketchup	15 mL	
10 oz.	can beef consommé	284 mL	
½ tsp.	salt	2 mL	
1 cup	sour cream	250 mL	
2 tbsp.	sherry	30 mL	

1. Mix the first 4 ingredients together well. Shape into meat balls. Arrange in a circular dish, (a pie dish works well) with the meatballs placed no more than 1 deep. Microwave on **HIGH** for 4 - 6 minutes or until the meatballs are just loosing their pink color. If you notice those around the outside of the dish are cooking more quickly than the ones in the center, re-arrange them halfway through the cooking time. (The cooked meatballs should go to the center of the dish while the undercooked ones should go around the outside.)

2. Drain the meatballs well, set aside. Freeze if desired.

3. Place the butter, mushrooms, onion and garlic in a medium-sized bowl. Microwave on **HIGH** for 3 - 4 minutes or until the onion is tender and transparent.

4. Mix in the flour, stirring well. Gradually add the ketchup and the beef consommé. Stir well. Microwave on **HIGH** for 2 - 4 minutes, stirring every 30 seconds, until the mixture has thickened and is just starting to boil. Cool slightly.

5. Add the salt, sour cream and sherry. Microwave on **HIGH** for 2 - 3 minutes until the mixture just returns to a boil. Cool slightly.

6. Add the drained meatballs to the sauce, and microwave until the mixture just returns to a boil. Serve over noodles or rice.

Serves 4 - 6. Recipe may be halved. Halve all ingredients and cooking times.

MACARONI AND HAMBURGER

This tasty casserole is a favorite in our household. It freezes well.

1	lb.	lean ground beef	450 g
1		large onion, finely chopped	1
½	tsp.	cinnamon	2 mL
½	tsp.	basil	2 mL
2		cloves garlic, crushed	2
¼	tsp.	pepper	1 mL
14	oz.	can tomato sauce	350 mL
5½	oz.	can tomato paste	156 mL
2	cups	uncooked macaroni	500 mL
1		egg	1
¼	cup	Parmesan cheese	50 mL
½	cup	butter or margarine	125 mL
¼	cup	flour	50 mL
2	cups	milk	500 mL
¼	tsp.	nutmeg	1 mL
¼	tsp.	salt	1 mL
¼	tsp.	pepper	1 mL
2		eggs, well beaten	2

1. Place hamburger and onion in a large bowl. Microwave on **HIGH** for 4 - 5 minutes or until the hamburger is just loosing its pink color. Stir frequently to break up the hamburger as it cooks. Drain well.

2. Add cinnamon, basil, garlic, pepper, tomato sauce and paste. Microwave on **MEDIUM** for 4 - 5 minutes or until the sauce is bubbly.

3. While microwaving the hamburger, cook the macaroni according to package instructions. (Although you can microwave pasta, it saves time to cook it on top of the stove while you are using the microwave to cook the meat sauce and the sauce). When the macaroni is tender, drain, rinse with cold water, and then mix with 1 egg.

4. Place half of the cooked macaroni in the bottom of a buttered 3-quart (3 L) casserole. Spread meat sauce on top of the macaroni, and then top with the remaining macaroni. Sprinkle with Parmesan cheese. Microwave for 5 minutes on **HIGH**.

5. Microwave butter or margarine in a medium-sized bowl for 1 - 2 minutes on **HIGH** or until it is completely melted.

6. Stir in flour. Mix well. Slowly add the milk, stirring well so that there are no lumps in the mixture. Microwave on **HIGH** for 3 - 4 minutes, stirring every 30 seconds, until the sauce thickens and just begins to boil.

MACARONI AND HAMBURGER (cont'd.)

7. Mix in spices. Pour a little of the hot sauce into the beaten eggs, mix well and pour this mixture back into the thickened sauce. Mix well.

8. Pour the custard over the microwaved meat and macaroni mixture. Sprinkle with additional Parmesan cheese if desired. Microwave on **MEDIUM** for 10 - 15 minutes or until the custard is set.

Serves 8. To halve recipe, halve times and ingredients.

OLD-FASHIONED RICE PUDDING

It is difficult to microwave the traditional custard-style rice pudding without it separating. In this easier version, cooked rice is added to a tasty cream sauce, and the results are terrific!

2½	cups	cooked white rice	625	mL
¼	cup	butter	50	mL
2	tbsp.	cornstarch	30	mL
¼	cup	brown sugar	50	mL
¼	tsp.	cinnamon	1	mL
⅛	tsp.	nutmeg	0.5	mL
2	cups	milk	500	mL
¼	cup	softened raisins*	50	mL
3		egg yolks	3	
		nutmeg for garnish		

1. In a medium-sized microwave bowl, microwave butter on **HIGH** for 1 minute. Stir in cornstarch, brown sugar, cinnamon and nutmeg.

2. Stir well. Gradually add milk and raisins. Microwave on **HIGH** for 3 - 4 minutes or until the mixture thickens. Stir every minute.

3. Add a little of the hot milk mixture to the beaten egg yolks. Mix well. Return the hot liquid/egg yolk mixture to the hot liquid. Stir well. Microwave for 1 - 2 minutes on **HIGH** or until the mixture just returns to a boil.

4. Stir in rice. Serve warm or cooled.

Serves 4 - 6 persons. Recipe may be halved. Halve all ingredients and cooking times.

* To soften raisins, microwave 1 cup (250 mL) of dried raisins with 1 tbsp. (15 mL) of rum or water for 1 minute on HIGH. Rum imparts a delicious flavor to the raisins, which are, in turn, a real asset to any recipe calling for them.

SOFT GINGERBREAD

This moist, dark cake can be served with lemon sauce or whipped cream and applesauce. Best if served warm.

½ cup	butter or margarine	125 mL
½ cup	white granulated sugar	125 mL
1	egg	1
½ cup	fancy molasses	125 mL
1½ cups	sifted all-purpose flour	375 mL
1 tsp.	baking soda	5 mL
1 tsp.	ground ginger	5 mL
¼ tsp.	cinnamon	1 mL
¼ tsp.	salt	1 mL
⅛ tsp.	ground cloves	0.5 mL
½ cup	boiling water	125 mL

1. Cream butter and sugar together in a large bowl, until light and fluffy. Add egg and beat well. Stir in molasses.

2. Sift together dry ingredients. Alternate adding dry ingredients and hot water to butter mixture.

3. Pour the batter into a straight-sided 9-inch (23 cm) circular, well-greased cake dish. Make sure the dish is no more than ½ full.

4. Microwave on **MEDIUM HIGH**, covered with a lid, inverted pie dish, or dinner plate, for 8 - 12 minutes or until the cake is just starting to pull away from the sides of the dish and a toothpick inserted in the centre comes out clean. Let stand for 3 - 4 minute and invert out of the dish.

5. Serve with Thick Lemon Sauce or whipped cream and applesauce.

Serves 6. Do not halve.

THICK LEMON SAUCE

1	egg, well beaten	1
½ cup	white granulated sugar	125 mL
	dash salt	
2 tbsp.	melted butter	30 mL
2	lemons, juice of	2

1. Combine all ingredients in a 2-cup (500 mL) measure. Microwave on **MEDIUM HIGH** for 1½ - 2½ minutes or until the mixture is thick and clear, stirring once.

TASTY APPLESAUCE

One of the Dam's favorites, this applesauce is nice and sweet and is best spread on hot-buttered toast or warm gingerbread. This particular rendition is adaptable to your own preference. All will enjoy the speed and ease of preparation.

5 - 6	cooking apples	5-6	
½ cup	water	125	mL
1 tbsp.	lemon juice	15	mL
½-1½ cups	white granulated sugar	125-375	mL
1 tsp.	cinnamon	5	mL
dash	nutmeg	dash	
½ tsp.	vanilla	5	mL

1. Wash and cut apples into quarters. Core. Cut each quarter in half. Place in a large bowl. Mix the lemon juice with the water and pour over the apples. If you are using older apples, add ¼ cup (50 mL) more water.

2. Microwave the apples for 5 - 8 minutes, covered, on **HIGH** or until the apples are tender. Strain apples through a strainer, or process in blender until puréed. Return to bowl.

3. Add enough sugar to make the sauce palatable. Microwave on **HIGH**, uncovered, for an additional 3 minutes.

4. Sprinkle with remaining ingredients. Adjust if necessary.

5. Applesauce may be stored in covered container in the refrigerator for up to 2 weeks.

Makes 3 cups (750 mL) of applesauce. Recipe may be halved. Halve all ingredients and cooking times.

For juicier citrus fruits, microwave each piece on HIGH for 30 seconds, or until the fruit is just beginning to feel warm to touch.

FRUIT NEWTONS

These terrific bars are unparalleled by any of Sir Isaac's inventions. Using some imagination, you can invent your own fillings (or use 1 of my favorites, listed below). Terrific for lunches and snacks.

1 cup	butter or margarine	250	mL
2 cups	packed brown sugar	500	mL
4	eggs	4	
2 tsp.	vanilla extract	10	mL
5 cups	all-purpose flour	1.25	L
1 tsp.	salt	5	mL
1 tsp.	baking powder	5	mL
3 - 4 cups	Fruit Filling (recipes follow)	750mL- 1	L

1. Beat together butter, sugar, eggs and vanilla until well blended.

2. Mix flour, salt, and baking powder. Stir into first mixture (dough will be stiff). Wrap in plastic wrap. Chill for 3 - 4 hours or overnight. By chilling the dough you will need much less flour to roll it out since it is less likely to stick to the surface.

3. When ready to bake, turn dough out on a lightly floured surface. Roll into a 14 x 12-inch (30 x 35 cm) rectangle. Do not roll too thin or the dough may split when filled. Cut into 4 strips 3½ x 12-inches (8.75 x 30 cm) long.

4. Spoon filling evenly down the centre of the strips. Turn in sides of strips over filling. Press edges together to seal. If desired, lightly moisten the area that will overlap with water prior to sealing. Cut each strip into 10 pieces. Arrange seamside down on a greased baking sheet.

5. Bake at 375°F (190°C) for 10 - 12 minutes or until firm and golden brown. Remove to racks to cool. Store in an airtight container.

FIG, DATE OR APRICOT FILLING

12 oz.	dried figs, dates or apricots	340	g
¼ cup	white granulated sugar	50	mL
¾ cup	water	175	mL
2 tbsp.	lemon juice	30	mL

1. Chop figs, dates or apricots. Mix in a small bowl with remaining ingredients.

FRUIT NEWTONS (cont'd.)

2. Microwave on **HIGH** for 5 - 8 minutes or until mixture is thick and jam-like. Stir twice, while microwaving. Cool slightly. Fill bars with a thin layer of filling.

Makes 2 cups (500 mL) of filling.

RASPBERRY OR BLUEBERRY FILLING

Raspberry is a real favorite in our family. Unfortunately , it is one of the most expensive to make.

15 oz.	frozen raspberries or blueberries	425
½ cup	white granulated sugar	125 mL
2 tbsp.	lemon juice	30 mL

1. Place all ingredients into a deep bowl.

2. Microwave on **HIGH** for 8 - 12 minutes or until the mixture is thick and jam-like. Stir frequently.

Makes 2½ cups (625 mL) of filling.

APPLE FILLING

Another popular filling, not quite as costly as the raspberry.

4	large cooking apples, peeled, cored	4
½ cup	white granulated sugar	125 mL
2 tbsp.	lemon juice	30 mL
¼ cup	water	50 mL
½ tsp.	cinnamon	2 mL
	dash nutmeg	

1. Place all ingredients into a deep bowl. Microwave on **HIGH** for 8 - 12 minutes or until the mixture is thick and jam like. Stir frequently. Cool and fill bars.

Makes 3 cups (750 mL) of filling.

2 cups (500 mL) crystallized honey can be clarified by microwaving on HIGH for 2 - 2½ minutes. Stir every 60 seconds. Store in an airtight container to prevent the honey from crystallizing again. Honey should not be refrigerated.

FRUIT CRISP

There are as many recipes for fruit crisp as there are orchards in British Columbia. This one is unique because it has a crust on both the bottom and the top.

1 cup	sifted all-purpose flour	250 mL
½ cup	quick cooking oatmeal	125 mL
¼ cup	graham cracker crumbs	50 mL
½ cup	melted butter or margarine	125 mL
1 cup	brown sugar	250 mL
1 tsp.	cinnamon	5 mL
½ cup	white granulated sugar	125 mL
1 cup	water	250 mL
2 tbsp.	cornstarch	30 mL
1 tsp.	vanilla	5 mL
4 cups	raw, chopped fruit (apples, rhubarb, cherries, blueberries,peaches) If you are using rhubarb, use 1 cup (250 mL) white sugar instead of ½ cup (125 mL).	1 L

1. Mix until crumbly, flour, oatmeal, graham cracker crumbs, melted butter or margarine, brown sugar and cinnamon. Press half of the crumb mixture into a well-greased 2-quart (2 L) casserole. For this recipe it is preferable to use a deep straight-sided casserole, so that the layers are not too thin.

2. Cover with layer of fruit.

3. Combine white sugar, water, cornstarch and vanilla in a medium-sized microwave-safe bowl. Microwave on **HIGH** for 1 - 2 minutes or until the mixture is thick and clear, stirring once. Pour over fruit. Top with remaining crumbs.

4. Microwave on **MEDIUM HIGH** for 8 - 10 minutes or until the fruit is fork tender. Serve warm with vanilla ice cream or whipping cream.

Serves 4 - 6. Do not halve recipe.

Nifty little kid pleasin' snacks can be made with a little leftover cake batter. Spoon 2 tbsp. (30 mL) of batter into the bottom of flat-bottomed ice cream cones. Microwave 6 cones for 1½ - 3 minutes on HIGH, or until the cake appears dry and completely cooked. Decorate with icing.

GRANOLA

This granola is not as dry and fine as some, and if stirred only once during microwaving it tends to cook in small chunks.

4 - 5 cups	large-flake oatmeal	1	L
1 cup	raw wheat germ	250	mL
½ cup	sesame seeds	125	mL
½ cup	shelled sunflower seeds	125	mL
½ cup	unsweetened, medium coconut	125	mL
⅓ cup	brown or demerara sugar	75	mL
½ tsp.	salt	2	mL
¾ cup	vegetable oil	175	mL
½ cup	water	125	mL
¾ cup	liquid honey	175	mL
1½ tsp.	pure vanilla extract	7	mL
½ cup	raisins	125	mL
½ cup	dried banana chips, optional	125	mL
½ cup	almonds, optional	125	mL

1. Combine the first 7 ingredients in a large bowl. Mix well.

2. Place vegetable oil, water, honey and vanilla in a blender. Blend for 15 seconds. Pour over the first 7 ingredients. Mix well so that the mixture is evenly coated.

3. Spread half of the mixture in a large, wide casserole or cooking tray and microwave on **MEDIUM** for 8 - 12 minutes or until the mixture is a light golden brown, stirring once. Repeat with the second half.

4. After microwaving, add raisins, dried banana chips and almonds, if desired. Cool and store in an air-tight container.

Makes approximately 8 cups (2 L) of granola. Recipe can be halved, although it stores well.

Make your own dried orange or lemon peel in the microwave oven. Sprinkle finely grated peel (do not include pith) from 1 orange or 2 small lemons in a circle on a paper-towel-covered plate. Microwave on HIGH for 2 - 3 minutes or until slightly dried. Toss and rearrange with fingers every 30 seconds. Cool until dry to touch, and store in an air-tight container.

THANKSGIVING

For anyone who enjoys cooking and entertaining, Thanksgiving Day provides an excellent opportunity to have some fun and delight guests with the ever-increasing variety of foods that this country has to offer. Fun you say?

Even to the most experienced entertainer, cooking for a crowd whether it be 8 or 20, can be overwhelming. The head "chef" never seems to get a chance to socialize, and by the time the meal is on the table, he or she is far too exhausted to enjoy the fruits (and vegetables) of his/her labor.

Thanks to the microwave, this can be improved. Here are 6 suggestions to help you have the most enjoyable and relaxing Thanksgiving ever, even if you are the "cook".

1. Prepare all vegetable dishes very early in the day, i.e. boil and mash potatoes; peel, slice and cook carrots; assemble casseroles (if you are having any) and bake until done. Chill finished dishes until ready to reheat. Approximately ¾ hour before serving, stack all casseroles in the microwave, covering each with a lid or dinner plate. Reheat on HIGH until all are piping hot. The flavor of the casseroles will be uncompromised even though the casseroles have been rewarmed. Since the vegetables are prepared when things are still unhurried, extra time can be devoted to your recipes to ensure perfection in everything from proper seasoning to attractive garnishes. As an added bonus, all the dirty pots and pans can be long gone by the time guests arrive.

2. If you are serving rolls with your meal, place them in a wicker basket lined with a paper napkin or a fancy cloth, a few hours before meal time. Cover with another napkin or cloth. Place the entire basket into a plastic bag until ready to warm. Just prior to sitting down for dinner, remove the plastic bag, then microwave on HIGH until the rolls just begin to feel warm. Do NOT microwave until they are piping hot. The timing varies considerably with the type of rolls. However, 15 seconds per roll should give you a rough idea of what timings to expect. This should be the last thing you reheat before seating yourself.

3. The turkey can be sliced early, and reheated just before the meal. If you have carved the turkey early, cover the slices with a single layer of lettuce leaves while reheating. This helps prevent the turkey from drying out and retains the rich flavor of the meat.

THANKSGIVING (cont'd.)

4. Turkey dressing can be prepared the evening before, refrigerated, and stuffed into the turkey JUST PRIOR to roasting.

5. Any turkey over 11 lbs. (5 kg) should be cooked conventionally to ensure even cooking. Smaller turkeys may be microwaved, although personally, I do not recommend it. My reasons for this are : (a) the skin, although it does brown somewhat, does not crisp; rather it becomes quite chewy; and (b) microwaving a turkey ties up your microwave oven for a considerable part of the day, when it could be used for vegetables, etc, and food items that microwave very well. If you plan to microwave a small turkey, sprinkle it with paprika for color and, halfway through the microwaving time, shield the tip of the breast bone and the tips of the wings and drumsticks with foil. The turkey should be completely thawed before microwaving or roasting. Microwave any turkey smaller than 11 lbs. (5 kg) for 8 minutes/ lb. (18 minutes/ kg) on MEDIUM HIGH. When done, the internal temperature of the turkey should be 170°F (77°C), after standing 15 minutes.

6. Whipping cream for pies, fancy coffees, etc. is difficult to do ahead of time, unless a stabilizer is used. Whipped cream can be set in a colander, in a bowl. Any cream separating will collect in the bowl, and can be used as coffee cream. Whipped cream can also be spooned in mounds onto a sheet of wax paper and frozen. Once frozen it can be stored in an airtight container. The Pumpkin Pie recipe on page 96 incorporates the whipped cream right into the pie, no need to whip cream at the last moment.

FRESH CRANBERRY SALAD

Although this recipe is not microwaved, it is super with a turkey dinner and can be almost completely prepared the evening before.

24 oz.	fresh cranberries	700	g
3 cups	white granulated sugar	750	mL
1	orange, juice of	1	
2 cups	red seedless grapes, halved	500	mL
1	pear, cored, diced	1	
¼ cup	walnuts, finely chopped	50	mL
1 cup	whipping cream, whipped	250	mL

1. Chop cranberries or grind in food processor. Add sugar and orange juice and let stand at room temperature overnight.

2. Drain cranberries after they have stood overnight. Add grapes, pear and walnuts to cranberries. Fold in whipped cream. Add additional sugar if a sweeter salad is desired. Refrigerate until ready to serve.

Serves 12. Recipe may be halved.

SVEA'S SUNSHINE SALAD

My mother prepares this salad every Thanksgiving and Christmas dinner. It is light and refreshing, and alway brings a welcome round of compliments.

3 cups	boiling water	750 mL
6 oz.	orange-flavored gelatin	170 g
8 oz.	cream cheese	250 g
1 tbsp.	mayonnaise	15 mL
1 tbsp.	lemon juice	15 mL
1 cup	fruit-flavored mini marshmallows	250 mL
	grapes, mandarin oranges for garnish	

1. Mix water and gelatin in a deep bowl. Stir until the gelatin is dissolved.

2. Place cream cheese on a small plate and microwave on **HIGH** for 30 seconds or until softened. Beat the cream cheese, mayonnaise and lemon juice into the hot gelatin mixture until it is light and frothy.

3. Cool until the mixture is just staring to gel. Fold in marshmallows and pour into a lightly greased gelatin mold. Chill until set.

4. When ready to serve, remove from mold and garnish with fruit.

Serves 8. May be halved. Use the small packages of gelatin and cream cheese.

CAULIFLOWER AND LEEK HOLLANDAISE

This is a spectacular dish, and easy to prepare. Make sure that you do not boil the Hollandaise Sauce.

1	medium cauliflower	1
3	leeks OR	3
6	green onions	6

HOLLANDAISE SAUCE:

1 tbsp.	water	15 mL
1 tbsp.	lemon juice	15 mL
	dash salt	
	dash white pepper	
3	egg yolks	3
1 cup	melted butter, cooled	250 mL
2 tbsp.	chopped parsley	30 mL

CAULIFLOWER AND LEEK HOLLANDAISE (cont'd.)

1. Trim cauliflower but leave it whole. Trim leeks or green onions, cut in 2-inch (5 cm) pieces. Place all vegetables in a 2-quart (2 L) casserole, cover.

2. Microwave for 5 - 8 minutes on **HIGH** until just tender. Do NOT over-microwave.

3. Make sauce. Mix the water, lemon juice, salt and pepper in a small microwave-safe bowl. Add the egg yolks and beat until thick. Microwave on **HIGH** for 1 - 2 minutes, whisking well after every 30 seconds until the mixture thickens.

4. Add cooled butter, bit by bit, whisk well after each addition. Microwave on **HIGH** for 30 seconds to 1 minute, until warm. DO NOT BOIL.

5. Arrange cauliflower and leeks or green onions on a hot serving dish. Pour sauce over the top. Sprinkle with parsley.

Serves 6. Do not halve.

SWEET POTATO SURPRISE

This recipe, from a wonderful friend in Colorado, is a tradition in our household every year.

1	large sweet potato	1	
2 tbsp.	butter	30	mL
2 tbsp.	orange juice	30	mL
2 tbsp.	brandy	30	mL
2 tbsp.	brown sugar	30	mL
½ cup	finely chopped pecans	125	mL
	salt and pepper to taste		
1 cup	marshmallows	250	mL

1. Pierce potato with a fork several times. Microwave on **HIGH** for 7 - 15 minutes or until the potato feels very soft. Cool slightly.

2. Peel the potato. Chop into chunks and place in a 1-quart (1 L) casserole. Mix in butter, orange juice, brandy and brown sugar. Beat until smooth. Fold in pecans. Season if desired. Smooth mixture and then sprinkle with marshmallows.

3. Microwave, uncovered for 3 - 4 minutes on **HIGH** or until the casserole is piping hot and the marshmallows are melted.

Serves 6. To serve 2-3, halve all cooking times and ingredients.

ELEGANT DRESSING

Simple to microwave, this traditional stuffing is an old-time family favorite.

1½ cups	chopped onion	375 mL	
1 cup	chopped celery, leaves included	250 mL	
¾ cup	butter or margarine	175 mL	
½ lb.	ground sausage meat	250 g	
½ cup	coarsely chopped mushrooms	125 mL	
8 cups	unseasoned bread crumbs	2 L	
1 tbsp.	salt	15 mL	
½ tsp.	freshly ground pepper	2 mL	
1 tsp.	sage	5 mL	
½ tsp.	thyme	2 mL	
½ tsp.	rosemary	2 mL	
½ tsp.	nutmeg	2 ml	
¼ cup	dry white wine	50 mL	
¾ cup	chicken broth	175 mL	
1	large egg, lightly beaten	1	
½ cup	dried apricots, chopped	125 ml	

1. In a small bowl, combine onion, celery and butter. Microwave on **HIGH** for 3 - 4 minutes or until the onions and celery are tender.

2. In a different bowl, combine sausage and mushrooms. Microwave on **HIGH** for 3 - 4 minutes or until the meat is no longer pink. Stir frequently to break up meat. Drain off any excess fat. Toss in onion and celery.

3. Combine mixture with bread crumbs and add seasoning. Moisten dressing with wine and/or chicken broth, add egg and apricots and mix well.

4. Stuff turkey just prior to roasting or microwave separately in a well-greased bowl on **MEDIUM** for 10 minutes.

Makes about 10 cups (2.5 L) of stuffing, or enough for a 20 lb (8 - 10 kg) turkey.

Warm bacon for easy separating. Microwave cold bacon, on a plate, removed from wrappings, for 30 seconds to 1 minute.

SUGARBUSH MOUNTAIN MAPLE MOUSSE WITH VANILLA CRÈME RUM SAUCE

If the more traditional Pumpkin Pie (see page 96) doesn't entice you or your family, I'm sure this will.

2	eggs, separated	2	
½ cup	pure maple syrup	125	mL
1 tsp.	maple extract	5	mL
¼ cup	dark brown sugar	50	mL
¾ tbsp.	unflavored gelatin	12	mL
¼ cup	cold water	50	mL
1 cup	whipping cream	250	mL
¾ tsp.	vanilla extract	4	mL
	Vanilla crème Rum Sauce *		

1. Combine egg yolks, maple syrup, maple extract and brown sugar in a deep, microwave-safe bowl. Microwave on **MEDIUM** for 3 - 5 minutes or until the mixture thickens and slightly coats the back of a spoon. Stir frequently.

2. Sprinkle gelatin over cold water and let set until softened. When softened, microwave on **HIGH** for 1 - 2 minutes or until the gelatin is completely dissolved.

3. Stir gelatin into the maple mixture, stirring constantly until it is incorporated. Let cool until the mixture mounds slightly when dropped from a spoon. (Do not place in freezer.)

4. Beat whipping cream until firm enough to hold its shape but not stiff. Beat in vanilla. With clean beaters, beat egg whites until fluffy soft peaks form. Gently whisk about ½ cup (125 mL) of the egg whites into the mousse mixture to lighten it, then fold in the remaining egg whites. Fold in the whipped cream.

5. Spoon mousse into molds about the size of a coffee cup, tapping mold gently on a flat surface to settle mousse and eliminate any air pockets. Refrigerate 2 - 4 hours or until set.

6. When ready to serve, run a thin sharp knife around the inner edge of the mold. Invert each mold onto individual serving plates. Ladle Vanilla Crème Rum Sauce, page 92, over Maple Mousse just before serving.

Serves 6. Do not halve.

*VANILLA CRÈME RUM SAUCE

1 cup	heavy cream	250 mL
1 cup	milk	250 mL
2 tbsp.	dark rum	30 mL
⅓ cup	white granulated sugar	75 mL
2	egg yolks	2
1 tsp.	vanilla	5 mL
2 tsp.	cornstarch	10 ml
	salt to taste	

1. Mix cream, milk and rum in a small, deep, microwave-safe bowl. Whisk ingredients well. Microwave on **HIGH** for 2 - 3 minutes or until the mixture is hot.

2. Whisk remaining ingredients together well. Add a little of the hot liquid to the beaten egg yolk mixture. Mix well. Slowly whisk egg mixture back into the remaining hot cream. Microwave on **MEDIUM** for 3 - 4 minutes or until the mixture thickens. Do not boil. Stir frequently.

3. Cool before serving as a topping for the Maple Mousse. If curdling does occur, simply strain sauce through a fine sieve before serving.

Makes 3 cups (750 mL) of sauce.

For delicately warmed and scented hand towels, sprinkle hand towel with a mixture of 1 cup (250 mL) water, 1 tbsp. (15 mL) lemon juice and 2 whole cloves. Microwave wet hand towels for 1 - 2 minutes on HIGH.

HALLOWE'EN

The tradition of Hallowe'en goes back thousands of years. The earliest that it is traced to is the Druids, an order of priests who lived in ancient times. They were very superstitious people who had believed that on October 31st, all the wicked people who had died came back to earth, often in animal shapes. The name Hallowe'en started in the eighth century when the Roman Catholic Church declared November 1st as All Saints Day. The day before was a hallowed evening, or Hallowe'en. The ancient pagan customs were still so popular, they were combined into this Christian feast day. It's no trick to stir up these taste-tempting treats tht are sure to please your youngsters. Even some of the adults will be sure to sneak a nibble or two.

COOKING PUMPKIN

Don't throw it away this year! After scaring all the ghosts and goblins that visit your house, cook up Mr. Jack-o'-lantern for some soup, pies, or a tasty cheesecake. Cooking pumpkin in the microwave is quick, simple and 'clean'.

Halve the carved pumpkin. Place one-half in the microwave, shell and all. Place the half shell on the floor of the oven. If you have a very large pumpkin, you may need to quarter it. Cover with waxed paper to help prevent drying. Microwave on **HIGH** for 5 - 15 minutes, or until mushy. Scoop cooked pumpkin out of rind. Drain thoroughly. Purée pulp in a food processor, then drain in a fine sieve for 15 minutes. One pound of raw pumpkin yields about 1 cup (250 mL) of purée.

Pumpkin seeds are also a tasty treat, however, they are best done in the conventional oven.

When removing a cover or microwave-safe plastic wrap from a dish that's been in the microwave oven, lift the far corner first so the steam escapes away from you.

CREAM OF PUMPKIN SOUP

This thick soup is filling, and served with warm bread and a tossed salad would be all that is required for a nourishing lunch or dinner.

4 cups	cubed, raw potato	1 L
⅓ cup	finely sliced onion	75 mL
¼ cup	water	50 mL
½ tbsp.	chopped green pepper	7 mL
¼ cup	butter or margarine	50 mL
2 tbsp.	all-purpose flour	30 mL
1¼ cups	water	300 mL
2½ cups	milk	625 mL
½ cup	brandy	125 mL
1½ cups	canned tomatoes, undrained	325 mL
¾ cup	cooked, sieved pumpkin	175 mL
1½ tsp.	salt	7 mL
¼ tsp.	pepper	1 mL
⅛ tsp.	Worcestershire sauce	0.5 mL
	grated Cheddar cheese	
	parsley	

1. Combine potatoes, onion, ¼ cup (50 mL) water and green pepper in a 3-quart (3 L) casserole. Cover to steam. Microwave 12 - 15 minutes on **HIGH** or until vegetables are tender and well-cooked.

2. Add butter to hot vegetables. Blend in flour.

3. Add water, milk, brandy, canned tomatoes, pumpkin, salt, pepper and Worcestershire sauce. Mash or purée in a blender if you prefer a smooth soup. Return to casserole. Microwave 10 - 12 minutes, uncovered, on **HIGH** until just below the boiling point. Ladle into bowls.

4. Sprinkle with cheese. Garnish with parsley.

5. This soup freezes well.

Serves 7 - 8.

See photograph on back cover.

To vent microwave-safe plastic wrap, simply fold a small edge back from the dish. Never puncture or slit the wrap, even slightly. This can become a large tear and interfere with cooking results.

PUMPKIN CHEESECAKE

If you're not fond of pumpkin pie, but like cheesecake, chances are you'll love this light fluffy dessert.

1¼ cups	gingersnap cookie crumbs	300 mL
⅓ cup	butter or margarine	75 mL
¾ cup	milk	175 mL
2 cups	prepared pumpkin	500 mL
1½ cups	packed brown sugar	375 mL
⅛ tsp.	salt	0.5 mL
¾ tsp.	ginger	4 mL
¾ tsp.	cinnamon	4 mL
¼ tsp.	nutmeg	1 mL
5	eggs, separated	5
3 tbsp.	unflavored gelatin (3 envelopes)	45 mL
⅓ cup	reconstituted orange juice	75 mL
1 cup	whipping cream	250 mL
2 tbsp.	icing (confectioner's) sugar	30 mL
2 cups	cream cheese, softened	500 mL

1. Combine cookie crumbs and butter in a large bowl. Microwave on **HIGH** for 1 minute or until the butter just begins to melt. Mix well.

2. Press into the bottom of a 9-inch (23 cm) springform pan. Set aside.

3. Microwave milk with pumpkin, brown sugar, salt and spices in a large bowl on **HIGH** for 3 - 4 minutes or until the mixture is hot.

4. Beat egg yolks until thick and lemon-yellow colored. Add a little of the hot mixture to the egg yolks, stir well and then pour the egg/pumpkin mixture into the hot pumpkin. Microwave on **MEDIUM HIGH** for 4 - 5 minutes, stirring frequently until the mixture thickens. Do not boil.

5. Soften gelatin in orange juice and add to hot custard. Stir until dissolved. Cool until it begins to thicken.

6. Beat egg whites until stiff, not dry. Fold into custard. Cool a little, but not until set. Whip cream and icing sugar until firm. Whip cream cheese until light and fluffy. Fold cream cheese into whipped cream. Fold this mixture into the pumpkin mixture. Pour into the springform pan. Chill until set.

Serves 8. To halve, halve all ingredients, and use a 6-inch (15 cm) springform pan. Halve the microwave times.

PUMPKIN PIE

This light and creamy pie is a pleasant variation of the heavier, more traditional pumpkin pie. The pie shell should be precooked before the filling is added. Although a pie crust can be cooked in the microwave, it will turn golden-brown baked conventionally.

¾ cup	homogenized milk	175 mL
2 cups	prepared pumpkin	500 mL
1½ cups	packed brown sugar	375 mL
⅛ tsp.	salt	0.5 mL
¾ tsp.	ginger	4 mL
¾ tsp.	cinnamon	4 mL
¼ tsp.	nutmeg	1 mL
5	eggs, separated	5
2 tbsp.	unflavored gelatin (2 envelopes)	30 mL
⅓ cup	freshly squeezed orange juice	75 mL
1½ cups	whipping cream	375 mL
⅓ cup	sugar	75 mL
10- inch	baked, pie shell	25 cm

1. Microwave milk with pumpkin, brown sugar, salt and spices on **HIGH** for 3 - 4 minutes, in a large bowl, or until the mixture is hot.

2. Beat egg yolks until thick and lemon-yellow colored. Add a little of the hot mixture to the egg yolks, stir well and then pour the egg yolk/ pumpkin mixture into the hot pumpkin. Microwave on **MEDIUM HIGH** for 4 - 5 minutes stirring frequently until the mixture thickens. Do not boil.

3. Soften gelatin in orange juice and add to hot custard. Stir until dissolved. Cool a little but not until stiff. Whip cream. Fold the 1/3 cup (75 mL) sugar into the whipped cream, then fold cream into pumpkin mixture. Whip egg whites until stiff peaks form. Fold into pumpkin mixture. Chill until very thick and then pour into baked pie shell. Chill.

Serves 6. Do not halve recipe.

See photograph on back cover.

HALLOWE'EN TREATS

POPPYCOCK

There is nothing quite like caramel corn at this time of year. A snap to make in the microwave, this treat is great.

¾ cup	popping corn kernels	175 mL
1⅓ cup	pecans	325 mL
⅔ cup	almonds	150 mL
½ cup	corn syrup (white or light)	125 mL
1⅓ cups	white granulated sugar	325 mL
1 cup	butter or margarine	250 mL
1 tsp.	vanilla	5 mL

1. Pop corn in a heavy pan, or hot-air popper. This amount of kernels should yield 2 quarts (2 L) of popped corn. Mix with nuts. Set aside.

2. Mix corn syrup, sugar, butter and vanilla in a large, microwave-safe bowl. Microwave on **HIGH** for 10 - 15 minutes, stirring occasionally, until it turns a caramel color. Add vanilla.

3. Pour over corn and nuts. Mix well. Spread on greased cookie sheet to cool and then break into pieces. Store in a covered plastic cotainer.

Makes 2 quarts (2 L) of caramel corn.

See photograph page 96A.

POPCORN BALLS

These can be made into mini jack-o'-lanterns. Use orange-flavored gelatin and form balls. Before completely cool, place pieces of gumdrops for the eyes, nose and mouth. Leaf-shaped gumdrops may be used for the top.

1 cup	light corn syrup	250 mL
½ cup	white granulated sugar	125 mL
3 oz.	package fruit-flavored gelatin	85 g
1 cup	coarsely chopped peanuts	250 mL
¾ cup	popcorn kernels, popped	175 mL

1. Combine corn syrup and sugar in a large deep bowl. Microwave, uncovered, for 4 - 5 minutes on **HIGH** or until the mixture comes to a rolling boil, stirring once.

2. Remove from the microwave and add gelatin, stirring until dissolved. Stir in peanuts and popcorn and mix well. When cool enough to handle, shape into balls with lightly buttered hands. Decorate as desired.

3. Wrap each ball in plastic wrap and tie with orange and black ribbon.

Makes 24 - 30 small popcorn balls. Do not halve.

See photograph page 96A.

CANDIED APPLES

This recipe should not be doubled, as the mixture cools quickly. If you wish to make more than 6 apples, start with a new batch.

6	medium apples	6	
6	wooden sticks	6	
2 cups	sugar	500 mL	
⅔ cup	light corn syrup	150 mL	
1 cup	water	250 mL	
	red food coloring		

1. Wash and dry apples. Remove stem from each and insert a wooden skewer securely in its place.

2. Place sugar, corn syrup and water in a deep bowl. Microwave on **HIGH** for 15 - 20 minutes or until the mixture boils rapidly and reaches 300°F (150°C). Do NOT leave a candy thermometer in the microwave if it is not a special microwave candy thermometer. No thermometer? Drop a little of the mixture into very cold water. When removed, it should crack when tapped sharply.

3. Remove from microwave, stir in food coloring to give a bright rosy color.

4. Place bowl in a large pan of hot water. Hold each apple by its skewer, dip into syrup until coated; place on a greased tray to harden. Work quickly.

5. Once hardened, the apples can be wrapped in plastic wrap. Special "crinkly" wrap can be purchased from grocery stores and specialty shops that assemble fruit baskets. Secure the wrap with a piece of red yarn.

Makes 6 apples. Do not halve or double.

See photograph page 96A.

FANTASTIC CREAMY FUDGE

This excellent recipe for fudge also makes a delicious Christmas gift, wrapped in brightly colored boxes or tins.

2 cups	white granulated sugar	500 mL
¾ cup	butter, do not substitute	175 mL
⅔ cup	evaporated milk	150 mL
1 cup	chocolate chips	250 mL
7 oz.	marshmallow cream	200 g
1 tsp.	vanilla	5 mL
1 cup	chopped nuts	250 mL

FANTASTIC CREAMY FUDGE (cont'd.)

1. Combine sugar, butter and milk in a deep 2-quart (2 L) bowl. Since the mixture boils vigorously, it is necessary to use a deep-enough bowl to prevent spillovers.

2. Microwave on **HIGH,** uncovered, 4½ - 5 minutes or until the mixture just begins to boil. Stir well. Microwave on **HIGH** an additional 5½ minutes.

3. Stir in chocolate chips, marshmallow cream, vanilla and nuts. Stir until smooth and creamy.

4. Pour into greased 12 x 8-inch (30 x 20 cm) baking dish and cool until set. Cut into small squares. Freezes well.

Makes 3 lbs (1.5 kg) of delicious, creamy fudge.

PEANUT BUTTER CREAM SQUARES

Universal favorites, peanut butter and jelly, make these tasty squares packed with kid appeal.

1 cup	flour	250 mL
½ tsp.	baking soda	2 mL
¼ cup	packed brown sugar	50 mL
3 cups	crisp rice cereal, such as Cocoa Puffs	750 mL
½ cup	butter or margarine	125 mL
8 oz.	cream cheese, softened	400 g
¼ cup	peanut butter	50 mL
2 tbsp.	brown sugar	30 mL
¼ cup	instant nonfat dry milk powder	50 mL
1	egg	1
1 tbsp.	lemon juice	15 mL
2 tbsp.	grape juice	30 mL

1. Combine flour with soda in a large bowl. Stir in ¼ cup (50 mL) brown sugar and 2½ cups (625 mL) of cereal. Add butter, mix until crumbly.

2. Press ⅔ of the crumb mixture in the bottom of an 8-inch (20 cm) microwave-safe baking dish.

3. Beat cream cheese with peanut butter and 2 tbsp. (30 mL) brown sugar until light and fluffy. Add dry milk, egg and lemon juice; beat well.

4. Spread over crumb base; dot with jelly. Sprinkle remaining crumb mixture and ½ cup (125 mL) of cereal over top. Pat gently.

5. Microwave on **MEDIUM,** uncovered, for 5 - 9 minutes or until the mixture is firm. Cool in pan. Cut into 12 bars.

Makes 12 bars. Do not halve.

JACK-O'-LANTERN BURGERS

Give a hearty Hallowe'en send-off to your band of merry masquer-aders.

8	cooked burgers	8
8	slices processed cheese	8
4	toasted hamburger buns	4

1. Cut jack-o'-lantern eyes, nose and mouth shapes out of each slice of cheese or allow for a little self-expression and have each youngster cut out the face for his or her burger. Place a cut-out cheese slice on each patty and put each patty on a bun.

2. Place all burgers on a platter and microwave on **HIGH** for 1 - 3 minutes or until cheese JUST begins to melt.

3. Serve open-faced on buns with condiments on the side.

Serves 4 - 6. May be halved. Microwave each burger for 15 - 20 seconds.

See photograph page 96A.

SPICED HOT APPLE CIDER

After a chilling night of trick-or-treating, this warm nutritious drink will be much appreciated.

2 qts.	apple juice	2 L
1	cinnamon stick	1
6	whole cloves	6
1 tsp.	whole allspice	5 mL
¼ cup	packed brown sugar	50 mL
8	orange slices	8

1. Combine all ingredients except orange slices in a large bowl. Microwave for 5 - 6 minutes on **HIGH**. Reduce power level to **MEDIUM** and microwave an additional 5 minutes to extract all the flavor from the spices.

2. Strain into mugs and garnish each with an orange slice.

Makes 8 servings, 1 cup each. Recipe may be halved. Halve all ingredients and microwave times.

See photograph page 96A.

CHRISTMAS

At Christmas, it is important to most of us to spread holiday cheer throughout the season with distinctive dinners, festive desserts, old-fashioned goodies and gifts from your kitchen. There is tremendous satisfaction and joy in spreading happiness through the gift of time and thoughtfulness.

LEMON CRUMB SQUARES

These squares remind me a little of a lemon meringue pie, without the meringue, and without the mess. Absolutely delicious.

1¼ cups	graham wafer crumbs	300 mL
⅓ cup	granulated white sugar	75 mL
½ cup	butter or margarine	125 mL
½ cup	all-purpose flour	125 mL
½ cup	fine, unsweetened coconut	125 mL

FILLING:

⅔ cup	granulated white sugar	150 mL
1	large egg	1
1½	lemons, juice and rind	1½
½ cup	fine, unsweetened coconut	125 mL

1. Combine, in a large bowl, all crust ingredients. Work together until crumbly. Press, gently, a large half of the crumb mixture into an un-greased 9 x 9-inch (23 cm) glass dish. The Corning-ware casserole with the rounded corners works well.

2. Whisk all filling ingredients together in a medium-sized bowl. Microwave on **MEDIUM** for 2 - 3 minutes, stirring every 30 seconds, until the mixture has thickened. Do not boil.

3. Pour thickened filling over the bottom layer. Spread reserved crumbs over the filling. Press lightly with hand. Microwave on **MEDIUM HIGH** for 4 - 6 minutes or until the top layer appears dry. It will crack slightly, and some of the filling may bubble up through the top layer. This does not affect the final product.

4. Cool and cut into squares. Freezes well.

Makes 24 squares.

CRANBERRY BARS

A delicious combination, very similar to matrimonial bars, except with a decorative ribbon of festive red through the centre.

1 cup	white sugar	250 mL
½ cup	reconstituted orange juice	125 mL
12 oz.	fresh or frozen cranberries	340 g
1¼ cups	all-purpose flour	300 mL
1½ cups	rolled oats	375 mL
1 cup	packed brown sugar	250 mL
1 tsp.	baking soda	5 mL
½ tsp.	salt	2 mL
1 cup	butter or margarine	250 mL

1. Mix sugar, orange juice and cranberries in a large bowl. Mix well.

2. Microwave, uncovered, on **HIGH** for 12 - 15 minutes or until the mixture thickens. It should no longer be runny.

3. Meanwhile, measure flour, oats, sugar, baking soda and salt into a large bowl. Cut the butter into these ingredients until crumbly.

4. Press half of the crumbs into a greased 9 x 9-inch (23 cm) glass pan. Press very gently, unless you plan to use a chisel later to remove it. Set aside.

5. Spread the cranberry mixture carefully over the crust. Sprinkle remaining crumbs over the top. Press down gently with your hand.

6. Microwave, uncovered, on **MEDIUM** until the surface appears some-what set. It will still appear wet. On cooling, the squares will crisp somewhat, so take care not to over microwave.

7. Cool slightly and cut into squares. Remove and freeze when completely cool.

Yields 24 squares.

To crisp snack foods such as chips and crackers, microwave 2 cups (500 mL) of these foods in a paper towel-lined basket for 45 - 60 seconds on HIGH.

DECORATIVE STRAWBERRIES

My grandmother always made these pretty confections part of her Christmas baking. As a child I didn't appreciate the way they brightened up a tray of squares, I rather favored them because they were sinfully sweet.

1½ cup	white granulated sugar	375	mL
⅓ cup	water	75	mL
⅔ cup	butter	150	mL
2 cups	skim milk (do not substitute)	150	mL
2 x 3 oz.	packages strawberry gelatin	170	g
1 cup	sweetened, long strand coconut	250	g
½ cup	butter icing, tinted green	125	mL

1. Mix sugar, water, butter and skim milk together in a large deep bowl. Microwave on **HIGH** for 25 - 30 minutes or until the mixture starts to thicken. NOTE: What you are in fact making here is sweetened condensed milk. The microwaved milk should be slightly thinner than the canned, sweetened condensed milk because, on cooling, it will thicken. If you wish to substitute 1 can (300 mL) of sweetened condensed milk for the sugar, water, butter and skim milk you may. It is less than half the cost to make it from scratch.

2. Cool the thickened milk mixture completely. If the mixture curdles, put it in a blender for 4 to 5 seconds before continuing.

3. Mix half of the strawberry gelatin and just enough coconut into the cooled milk mixture so that you can form small balls that hold together well. The mixture will feel slightly sticky.

4. Roll the small balls in the remaining gelatin powder and then shape into strawberries. The resulting confection should be the same size as a medium-sized "real" strawberry.

5. Air dry the strawberries for a couple of hours, and then pipe green icing onto the top of the berry using a leaf tip, or spoon the icing onto the top of each berry so that it resembles a leaf.

6. Carefully place in an airtight container and freeze until needed.

Yields 25 strawberries.

GINGER SHORTBREAD

One of my grandmother's recipes, this shortbread is made with brown sugar and is darker in color than Scottish shortbread so that the lack of browning is not noticeable. Be sure to use candied ginger and not powdered.

1 cup	butter	250 mL
2 cups	all-purpose flour	500 mL
½ cup	brown sugar	125 mL
¼ cup	finely chopped candied ginger	50 mL
	diced candied fruit or maraschino cherries for garnish.	

1. Mix butter, flour, sugar, and ginger together. Beat until it is the consistency of putty.

2. Press the dough into a greased, glass, 9 or 10-inch (25 cm) pie dish. Smooth gently with the palm of your hand.

3. Using the tines of a dinner fork, gently press a border around the outside edge of the dough.

4. Place small pieces of candied fruit around the inside edge of the marks made with the fork.

5. Microwave on **MEDIUM** for 8 - 12 minutes or until the shortbread appears set. It will still be soft. The shortbread will crisp as it cools.

6. While still warm, cut into wedges, much like VERY slender pieces of pie. Cool completely and remove from the pan. Freezes well.

Yields approximately 40 wedges.

Dry and crisp wonton skins, turning them into dip chips. Cut 3 wonton skins diagonally into quarters. Arrange in a circle on a plate. Microwave on HIGH for 1 - 3 minutes or until lightly browned, rotating every 45 seconds.

CHICAGO CHEESECAKE BARS

These squares have been made all-time family favorites in our family by Aunt Meggie. They are easy to prepare and super quick in the microwave.

CRUST:

⅓ cup	butter or margarine	75 mL
⅓ cup	packed brown sugar	75 mL
1 cup	all-purpose flour	250 mL

FILLING:

8 oz.	cream cheese	250 g
¼ cup	granulated white sugar	50 mL
1	egg	1
1 tbsp.	lemon juice	15 mL
¼ cup	chopped red maraschino cherries	50 mL
¼ cup	green maraschino cherries	50 mL

1. Mix crust ingredients together until crumbly. Press all but ½ cup (125 mL) of the crumbs gently into the bottom of a 9 x 9-inch (23 cm) glass dish. Microwave on **HIGH** for 3 minutes.

2. Beat the cream cheese, white sugar, egg and lemon juice until light and fluffy. Fold in diced maraschino cherries. (These should be well-drained).

3. Pour over the prepared crust. Top with reserved crumbs. Microwave, uncovered, on **MEDIUM** for 6 - 10 minutes or until filling is set and a knife inserted into the center comes out clean. Cut into squares while still warm. Refrigerate or freeze until ready to use.

Yields 24 squares.

Cool cakes, in their dish, directly on a heat-proof countertop or other solid surface rather than a rack. This way the bottom of the cake will cook completely as the dish and countertop will conduct the heat better.

MATRIMONIAL BARS

These squares need no introduction, and are super when micro-waved.

CRUMB LAYER:

1¼ cups	all-purpose flour	300	mL
1½ cups	rolled oats	375	mL
1 cup	packed brown sugar	250	mL
1 tsp.	baking soda	5	mL
½ tsp.	salt	2	mL
1 cup	butter or margarine	250	mL

FILLING:

½ lb.	dates, cut up	250	g
½ cup	granulated white sugar	125	mL
⅔ cup	crushed pineapple, undrained	150	mL
1 tbsp.	lemon juice	15	mL

1. Measure flour, oats, sugar, baking soda and salt into a large bowl. Cut the butter into these ingredients until crumbly. Press half of the crumbs into a greased 9 x 9-inch (23 cm) glass pan. Press very GENTLY. Set aside.

2. In a large bowl combine the filling ingredients. Microwave on **HIGH** for 4 - 5 minutes, stirring occasionally, or until the dates are completely softened, or mushy.

3. Spread the date mixture carefully over the crust. Sprinkle remaining crumbs over the top. Press down gently with your hand.

4. Microwave, uncovered, on **MEDIUM**, 6 - 9 minutes, until the surface appears wet and shiny.

5. Cool and cut into squares.

Yields 24 squares.

RUM BALLS

There isn't much microwaving to these, but if you can microwave the chocolate prior to dipping, it does save on time and cleanup. Another of my grandmother's recipes, this is fun to make with a friend or child.

2 cups	mixed fruit	500 mL
2 tbsp.	rum, first amount	45 mL
½ cup	butter or margarine	125 mL
1 cup	icing or powdered sugar	250 mL
2 tbsp.	rum, second amount	45 mL
1 cup	sweetened, medium coconut	250 mL

DIP:

8 oz.	semisweet chocolate squares	225 g
⅓ cup	grated paraffin wax	75 mL
2 tbsp.	butter or margarine	45 mL
1 cup	whole pecans	250 mL

1. Pour the first amount of rum over fruit and microwave on **HIGH** for 2 - 3 minutes or until the fruit is warmed throughout. Cool completely. Drain before using if mixture is runny.

2. Cream butter and icing sugar. Mix in second amount of rum, coconut and drained fruit.

3. If mixture is runny, add a little extra icing sugar. Put mixture in freezer until hard enough to form bite-sized balls. Roll into balls and place on a cookie sheet. Place back in freezer until ready to dip.

4. To make dip, place squares, wax and butter into a deep narrow bowl. Microwave on **HIGH** for 2 - 3 minutes, stirring twice, until the chocolate is completely melted. Do not boil.

5. Dip balls in the chocolate using toothpick, allowing excess chocolate to drip off. Place on waxed paper and immediately place pecan on toothpick hole.

6. If you do not have enough chocolate for dipping, dip remaining balls in icing sugar. Actually, these are a nice contrast with the chocolate-dipped balls.

Yields 40 balls.

Melt chocolate squares for baking without a double boiler. Microwave 1 or 2 squares baking chocolate in a small glass dish for 2 - 3 minutes on MEDIUM until soft enough to stir.

CHOCOLATE PEPPERMINT BAR

This is one of my favorites come Christmas time. Its 3 layers are really attractive, with the green layer rippling through the centre.

BASE:

½ cup	butter or margarine	125	mL
2	squares unsweetened chocolate	2	
2	eggs	2	
1 cup	white granulated sugar	250	mL
1 tsp.	salt	5	mL
½ tsp.	peppermint extract	2	mL
½ cup	all-purpose flour	125	mL

MIDDLE LAYER:

1 cup	icing or powdered sugar	250	mL
2 tbsp.	butter or margarine	45	mL
1 tbsp.	milk	15	mL
1 tsp.	vanilla extract	5	mL
	few drops green food colouring		

TOP LAYER:

2	squares semisweet chocolate	2	
2 tbsp.	butter or margarine	30	mL

BASE:

1. Place butter and chocolate in a small bowl. Microwave on **HIGH** for 1 - 2 minutes or until the chocolate is melted. Stir every 30 seconds. Add beaten eggs. Beat well. Add sugar, salt, peppermint and flour. Beat well.

2. Pour batter into a greased 9 x 9-inch (23 cm) glass pan. Microwave, covered with a lid or pie plate, on **MEDIUM HIGH** for 4 - 5 minutes, or until the surface of the dough no longer appears wet. Do NOT overcook. Cool.

MIDDLE LAYER:

3. Mix sugar and butter until smooth. Add remaining ingredients and mix well. Spread on first layer (base) and cool until firm.

TOP LAYER:

4. Melt chocolate and butter together in the microwave on **HIGH** for 1 - 2 minutes.

5. Cool slightly and drizzle over the second layer. Cool this slightly and then cut into squares. If you wait until the squares have cooled completely the chocolate top layer cracks when cut.

Yields 24 squares.

CHICKEN IN SWEET-SOUR SAUCE

This excellent hors d'oeuvre can also be prepared for an elegant meal by substituting 4 - 6 chicken breasts for the mini drumettes.

3 lbs.	chicken drumettes (chicken wings, disjointed)	1.5 kg

SAUCE:

½ cup	cider vinegar	125 mL
½ cup	brown sugar	125 mL
½ cup	pineapple juice	125 mL
2 tbsp.	ketchup	30 mL
2 tbsp.	soy sauce	30 mL
¼ tsp.	paprika	1 mL
14 oz.	can pineapple chunks, drained, reserve liquid	398 mL
2 tbsp.	cornstarch	30 mL

1. Place chicken drumettes on a large plate or a roasting rack, so that the thick part of the drumette is towards the outside of the plate and the smaller part faces inward.

2. Cover loosely with waxed paper and microwave on **HIGH** for 20 - 24 minutes, or until the meat is no longer pink next to the bone. Set aside.

3. Start assembling sauce. Mix vinegar, sugar, pineapple juice and ketchup in a medium-sized bowl. Microwave, uncovered, on **HIGH** for 3 - 4 minutes or until the sauce just begins to boil.

4. Add soy sauce and paprika. Mix cornstarch with the reserved liquid from the pineapple chunks. Add to the hot liquid. Microwave on **HIGH** for an additional 2 - 3 minutes or until the mixture boils and thickens. Stir frequently.

5. Add the chicken drummettes, and pineapple chunks. Microwave, uncovered for an additional 3 - 4 minutes on **HIGH**, or until the mixture is piping hot.

Serves 8. For 4 servings: Halve all of the ingredients and cooking times. This sauce is also excellent with meatballs, and ham chunks.

SESAME - SOUR CREAM MEATBALLS

A subtle hint of ginger adds a new dimension to these excellent meatballs.

1½ lbs.	lean ground beef	750 g	
⅔ cup	finely chopped onion	150 mL	
½ cup	bread crumbs	125 mL	
1	egg	1	
¼ cup	milk	50 mL	
½ tsp.	salt	2 mL	
⅛ tsp.	black pepper	0.5 mL	
⅛ tsp.	powdered ginger	0.5 mL	

SESAME - SOUR CREAM SAUCE:

2 tbsp.	butter or margarine	30 mL
2 tbsp.	all-purpose flour	30 mL
¼ tsp.	salt	1 mL
½ tsp.	ginger	2 mL
½ cup	beef broth	125 mL
1 tbsp.	soy sauce	15 mL
2 tbsp.	toasted sesame seeds	30 mL
¾ cup	sour cream or plain yogurt	175 mL

1. Mix beef, onion, bread crumbs, egg, milk, salt, black pepper and ginger. Shape mixture into 1-inch balls.

2. Place meatballs on a large platter, or a circular roasting rack if you have one. Microwave, on **MEDIUM HIGH**, for 8 - 10 minutes, or until the meatballs are no longer pink.

3. Sauce preparation: Place butter in a small, deep bowl. Microwave on **HIGH** for 1 minute, or until the butter is completely melted. Blend in flour, salt and ginger.

4. Mix in beef broth. Stir well. Microwave on **HIGH** for 1 - 3 minutes or until the mixture thickens, and boils for 30 seconds. Add soy sauce and toasted sesame seeds.

5. Mix in sour cream. Pour sauce over the meatballs, and sprinkle the top with some additional sesame seeds if desired. If reheating take care not to boil the sour cream sauce as it may curdle.

Makes 40 cocktail-size meatballs.

NIPPY HORSERADISH DIP

This creamy dip is just slightly reminiscent of the flavor of horse-radish. Even those not really fond of horseradish will love its surprising smooth and creamy qualities.

½ cup	grated, sharp Cheddar cheese	125 mL
½ cup	cream cheese	125 mL
½ cup	mayonnaise (not salad dressing)	125 mL
¼ cup	prepared horseradish	50 mL
¼ cup	sour cream	50 mL

1. Mix the grated cheese and cream cheese in a small bowl. Microwave, uncovered, on **HIGH** for 45 seconds - 1½ minutes or until the cheese just begins to melt. Do not over microwave. Stir until creamy.

2. Mix in mayonnaise, horseradish and sour cream. Turn into serving bowl and let stand for at least 30 minutes for flavors to blend. Serve with crackers or raw vegetables.

Makes 2 cups (500 mL) of dip.

BACON AND PARMESAN-STUFFED MUSHROOM CAPS

After trying these at a friend's house years ago, they have become one of my personal favorites. Excellent as an hors d'oeuvre or as a vegetable dish.

15	large mushrooms	15
1	small onion, finely diced	1
6 slices	bacon, diced	6
¼ cup	Parmesan cheese	50 mL
¼ cup	bread crumbs	50 mL

1. Remove stems from mushrooms and chop finely. Add to onion and bacon and microwave on **HIGH** for 6 - 8 minutes, or until bacon is crumbly and onions are transparent. Stir frequently to break up bacon.

2. Add Parmesan cheese and bread crumbs. Mix well.

3. Stuff each mushroom cap with a heaping spoonful of this mixture.

4. Place in the bottom of a pie dish. Microwave, uncovered, on **HIGH** for 3 - 4 minutes or until the mushroom caps are tender.

Serves 7 - 8 people, 2 mushrooms each.

LIQUID HAND SOAP

Liquid hand soap is rather costly. The price of this homemade version is less than one-quarter of the cost of the manufactured product.

1 bar	soap with moisturizing cream*	140 g	
3 cups	water	750 mL	
	perfume, optional		

1. Grate the soap with a hand grater.

2. Mix soap, water and the moisturizing cream if using, in a large bowl. Microwave on **HIGH** for 4 - 7 minutes or until the mixture JUST comes to a boil and the soap dissolves. Don't worry if the mixture looks thin - it thickens as it cools. Add perfume if you are using it. Pour into dispensers.

*If the soap doesn't have moisturizing cream then add ¼ cup (50 mL) of your favorite brand. For a unique gift, use unscented soap and moisturizing cream. Include a note instructing the recipient to add a few drops of their favorite scent.

MICROWAVED PLAY DOUGH

I recently was asked to make this play dough while volunteering at my son's E.C.S. class. I was thrilled with the results. It's the best consistency that I've seen with play dough, and the kids had lots of fun helping me with it.

2 cups	all-purpose flour	500 mL	
1 cup	salt	250 mL	
1 tbsp.	alum	15 mL	
1½ cups	water	475 mL	
	food coloring		
1 tbsp.	vegetable oil	15 mL	

1. Mix all ingredients together in a large microwave-safe bowl. Add the food coloring to the water before adding to the rest of the ingredients, for even mixing.

2. Microwave on **HIGH** for 3 - 4 minutes, or until the mixture thickens. Stir after every minute.

3. This will keep in the refrigerator for several weeks. Cover tightly.

Makes enough for 1 cup (250 mL) portions of 3 different colors.

NEW YEAR'S EVE PARTY

Clockwise From Foreground

HOMEMADE MINCEMEAT

For those of us accustomed to thinking of mincemeat as the weird amber-colored goo that comes in jars from the supermarket, this is a sweet and savory surprise. It is meat, and it tastes like meat, but sweet. What a strange, old-fashioned harmony of flavors. Mincemeat is delicious warm, on ice cream or in individual tarts.

1 lb.	lean ground sirloin	450 g
½ cup	apple cider	125 mL
½ lb.	dry beef suet, pulverized	250 g
5 cups	tart apples, peeled and finely chopped	1.2 L
4 cups	seedless raisins	1 L
3 cups	currants	750 mL
2 cups	brown sugar	500 mL
1	lemon, juice of	1
2 cups	apple cider	500 mL
1 cup	amber rum	250 mL
1 tbsp.	cinnamon	15 mL
1½ tsp.	nutmeg	7 mL
1½ tsp.	ground cloves	7 mL
1½ tsp.	allspice	7 mL
2 tsp.	salt	10 mL

1. Place meat and ½ cup (125 mL) cider in a large microwave safe bowl and microwave on **MEDIUM** for 20 - 30 minutes or until the cider is completely absorbed.

2. Combine meat with all other ingredients. Mix thoroughly and microwave on **MEDIUM** for 15 minutes, adding more apple cider, if necessary, to keep the mixture loose, but not watery.

3. Cover and refrigerate for 1 - 3 days. Use as you would the more familiar canned mincemeat.

Makes enough mincemeat for 4 pies. Do not halve.

Warm hand lotion or baby oil in a plastic container with the lid off. Microwave on HIGH for 15 - 45 seconds. Shake or mix well before applying.

Make new lip gloss. Scrape remaining lipstick stubs into small glass bowl. Add an equal amount of petroleum jelly or leftover lip glaze. Microwave on HIGH for 20 - 60 seconds, stirring every 20 seconds with a wooden tooth pick until smooth.

CANDIED CITRUS PEEL

Citrus peel is an excellent garnish, as well as a tasty snack.

1 large	bright-skinned orange	1
2 cups	white granulated sugar	500 mL
¼ cup	water	50 mL

1. Using a very sharp paring knife, remove rind only from the orange. Do not peel off any of the bitter white pith.

2. Combine sugar and water in a microwave-safe bowl. Microwave on **HIGH** for 5 minutes or until the mixture comes to a boil. Add peel. Microwave on **LOW** for an additional 30 minutes. Let mixture cool and then remove peel from syrup. Let harden on waxed paper, parchment or aluminum foil. Can be stored in the freezer indefinitely, tightly covered.

Makes 2 cups (500 mL) of peel.

PEANUT BRITTLE

In 9 minutes!

1 cup	raw peanuts	250 mL
1 cup	white granulated sugar	250 mL
½ cup	white corn syrup	125 mL
⅛ tsp.	salt	0.5 mL
1 tsp.	butter	5 mL
1 tsp.	vanilla extract	5 mL
1 tsp.	baking soda	5 mL

1. Stir together peanuts, sugar, syrup and salt in a 2-quart (2 L) bowl. Microwave on **HIGH** for 7 - 8 minutes, stirring well after 4 minutes. If roasted salted peanuts are used, omit salt and add peanuts after the first 4 minutes of cooking.

2. Add butter and vanilla to syrup, blending well. Return to microwave and microwave for an additional minute on **HIGH**. Peanuts will be lightly browned and the syrup very hot.

3. Add baking soda and gently stir until light and foamy. Pour and spread mixture quickly onto lightly greased cookie sheet; let cool on half hour. When cool, break into small pieces. May be stored in an air-tight container.

Makes 1 lb. Do not Halve.

Variation: 1 cup (250 mL) pecan halves or 1 cup (250 mL) sesame seeds may be substituted for the peanuts.

OYSTER STEW

In many families, Oyster Stew is as much a part of Christmas as tinsel. This tasty stew takes only 7 minutes to microwave.

4 tbsp.	butter	60 mL
½ tsp.	Worcestershire sauce	2 mL
½ tsp.	celery salt	2 mL
¼ cup	minced green onion tops	50 mL
2 cups	oysters, drained, reserve liquid	500 mL
13 oz.	evaporated milk	400 mL
1 tsp.	salt	5 mL
¼ tsp.	white pepper	1 mL
	paprika	
	sprigs of parsley	

1. Place butter, Worcestershire sauce, celery salt, onions and oysters in a 3-quart (3 L) dish. Microwave on **HIGH** for 3 minutes or until the oysters just start to curl around the edges.

2. Add oyster liquid, milk, salt and pepper. Microwave on **HIGH** for 4 minutes. Stir once.

3. Sprinkle with paprika and serve with parsley.

Serve 4 - 5.

To microwave scallops place 1 lb. (450 g) in a single layer in a glass pie plate; cover with wet paper towel and microwave on HIGH for 4 - 6 minutes or until the scallops are opaque in color.

To clean a browning dish, sprinkle with baking soda. Scrub lightly. Rinses clean. For hard to remove stains mix ¼ cup (50 mL) of bleach with ¼ cup (50 mL) water. Soak for 2 - 3 hours. Rinse well.

WESTERN TOURTIÈRE

Straying from a traditional meat-only pie: grated celery, carrots and potato have been added. The spices are all optional and the amounts may vary with your preference. Savory, although not in this recipe, is a popular spice for tourtière in other recipes.

1 lb.	lean ground beef	500 g
1 lb.	ground pork	500 g
½ lb.	chicken, cooked, finely diced	250 g
1	medium onion, finely diced	1
1	stalk celery, finely chopped	1
1	medium potato, grated	1
1	medium carrot, grated	1
¼ tsp.	rosemary	1 mL
½ tsp.	allspice	2 mL
⅛ tsp.	cloves	0.5 mL
1 tsp.	sage	5 mL
⅛ tsp.	thyme	0.5 mL
⅛ tsp.	pepper	0.5 mL
¼ tsp.	salt	1 mL
½ cup	water	125 mL
2	eggs, well beaten	2
	dough for 2x9-inch (22 cm) pies	

1. Mix the meats and vegetables together in a large bowl. Microwave on **HIGH** for 6 - 7 minutes or until the meat is no longer pink, stirring and breaking up the meat very frequently. If you have a microwave colander, use it for this step, as the fat will all drip away from the meat. If you don't have a colander, drain the meat and vegetables very thoroughly.

2. Add the spices and the water to the well-drained meat and vegetables. Stir well. Microwave, covered, on **HIGH** for 15 minutes, stirring every 5 minutes. Adjust seasonings. Mix in 2 well-beaten eggs.

3. While the meat and vegetables are simmering, prepare the bottom pie crusts. Place in 2 x 9-inch (22 cm) pie dishes.

4. Split filling evenly between 2 pie shells. Cover with top crust. Use scraps of dough to make a Christmas cut-out for top of pie.

5. Brush the top of the pie with beaten egg yolk or milk. Bake at 450°F (230°C) for 5 minutes and reduce oven temperature to 350°F (180°C) and bake 15 - 20 minutes or until pastry is nicely browned.

Tourtières can be made ahead and frozen. Freeze, unbaked. Thaw completely before baking. To reheat Tourtière, microwave for 4-5 minutes on high. Yields 2 x 9-inch (22 cm) pies, each serves 10.

See photograph on front cover.

MOM'S FRUIT RELISH

Tourtière should be served with fruit or tomato relish. This is excellent, and is also great with meat loaf, macaroni and cheese, roast beef and mashed potatoes.

4 cups	diced, fresh tomatoes	1 L
1	medium onion, finely chopped	1
1	peach, peeled and chopped*	1
1	pear, peeled and chopped*	1
½ cup	finely chopped green pepper	125 mL
½ cup	finely chopped celery	125 mL
1	apple, peeled and chopped	1
½ cup	cider vinegar	125 mL
1 tsp.	salt	5 mL
⅓ cup	pickling spices, wrapped in cheesecloth	75 mL
½ cup	packed brown sugar	125 mL

1. Combine all of the above ingredients in a large bowl. Microwave, uncovered, on **HIGH** for 5 - 6 minutes or until the mixture comes to a boil.

2. Reduce the power level to **LOW** and microwave an additional 30 minutes to allow the flavor a chance to fully develop.

3. Remove the pickling spices. Pour into a large sterilized jar. Cover with a lid and keep in the refrigerator.

*The small dessert cans of fruit, drained, can be used if fresh fruit is not available. Makes 3 - 4 cups (750 mL - 1L).

Roasting chestnuts is simple and quick in the microwave oven, although not quite as traditional. To my knowlege there is no song written about it yet! Slit 1½ - 2 dozen chestnuts. Place in a single layer in a shallow microwave-safe dish. Microwave on HIGH for 2 minutes, turning over after 1 minute. Do not cover. Stir well. Microwave for 1 - 2 minutes more on HIGH or until the chestnuts are soft when squeezed. Let stand. Serve warm. If cooled completely reheat on HIGH for 30 seconds.

PLUM PUDDING

A plum pudding is rich in flavor, color and takes a fraction of the time it would to steam conventionally. Prepare it early so that it has time to mellow after being sprinkled with brandy.

1 cup	all-purpose flour	250 mL
2 cups	dry bread crumbs	500 mL
1⅓ cups	lightly packed brown sugar	325 mL
¾ pound	suet	365 g
¼ tsp.	salt	2 mL
⅛ tsp.	ginger	0.5 mL
¼ tsp.	mace	1 mL
½ tsp.	cinnamon	2 mL
½ tsp.	nutmeg	2 mL
⅓ cup	granulated white sugar	75 mL
1½ cups	dried prunes	375 mL
1½ cups	raisins	375 mL
½ cup	mixed peel	125 mL
5	medium eggs	5
1 cup	brandy	250 mL
	Additional brandy to drizzle over steamed puddings.	

1. Mix flour, crumbs, 1⅓ cups (325 mL) sugar, suet, salt, and spices together.

2. Mix ⅓ cup (75 mL) sugar with prunes, raisins and mixed peel. Add to the flour mixture.

3. Slightly beat the eggs and add to the mixture. Finally mix in the brandy.

4. Divide the mixture in half and pour each half of the mixture into a well-greased 1-quart (1 L) bowl. A Pyrex bowl with scalloped edges works well, and the resulting puddings have a really attractive shape.

5. Cover the bowl tightly with a microwave-safe plastic wrap. Cover with a lid or a plate. Each pudding will now be covered with both microwave-safe plastic wrap and a lid. Place the bowl in another bowl of water, which is deep enough to cover half of the bowl that the plum pudding is in.

6. Place BOTH sets of bowls in the microwave. Microwave on **HIGH** for 15 minutes. Microwave an additional 20 - 35 minutes on **MEDIUM** or until the pudding is firm and a skewer inserted in the centre comes out clean. If you cannot fit both puddings in at one time, microwave one for HALF of the times given above.

PLUM PUDDING (cont'd.)

7. Cool, remove from the bowls and drizzle with brandy. Wrap well and freeze until needed.

8. When ready to serve, defrost, and microwave on **MEDIUM**, uncovered for 5 - 6 minutes or until warmed throughout.

9. If you wish to flame the pudding before serving, warm the brandy (about 2 - 3 tablespoons (30 - 45 mL)) for 15 - 20 seconds on **HIGH**. Pour over the steamed, warmed pudding and ignite.

10. Pudding may be served with Creamy Hard Sauce and Lemon Sauce or Brandy Sauce.

Serves 10 - 12. Recipe may be halved. Be sure to halve your cooking times.

CREAMY HARD SAUCE

1 cup	sweet butter	250 mL
3 cups	icing or powdered sugar	750 mL
2 tsp.	brandy	10 mL
2	egg yolks, beaten	2
¼ tsp.	nutmeg	1 mL
	waxed paper	
	maraschino cherries	

1. Cream butter and sugar together until light and fluffy.

2. Mix in remaining ingredients, except cherries. Pipe small mounds onto a piece of waxed paper on a cookie sheet. Top each with a cherry.

3. Freeze. When frozen, pack into an airtight container and keep frozen until needed.

4. Place hard sauce on a piece of warmed Plum Pudding and top with warmed Lemon Sauce.

Makes enough Hard Sauce for 10 people.

HOT LEMON SAUCE

½ cup	butter or margarine	125 mL
1 cup	granulated white sugar	250 mL
1 tbsp.	cornstarch	15 mL
1 tbsp.	grated lemon peel	15 mL
⅓ cup	lemon juice	75 mL
⅓ cup	water	75 mL
2	eggs, slightly beaten	2

1. Cream butter, sugar and cornstarch. Blend in remaining ingredients.

2. Microwave on **HIGH** for 3 - 6 minutes, or until clear, stirring frequently. Sauce may be made ahead and reheated. Do not freeze.

Makes 2 cups (500 mL) of sauce.

BRANDY SAUCE

One of my favorites, which may be used as an alternative to Hard Sauce and Lemon Sauce.

½ cup	packed brown sugar	125 mL
2 tbsp.	cornstarch	45 mL
1½ cups	milk	375 mL
¼ cup	melted butter	50 mL
⅛ tsp.	nutmeg	0.5 mL
1 tsp.	molasses	5 mL
¼ cup	brandy	50 mL

1. In a small bowl measure sugar and cornstarch.

2. Whisk in milk, butter, nutmeg and molasses.

3. Microwave on **HIGH** for 4 - 6 minutes or until thickened, stirring every minute.

4. Add brandy, and serve. May be made ahead and reheated.

Makes 2 cups (500 mL) of sauce.

ORANGE-BRANDY LIQUEUR

Easy to make, and surprisingly similar to the ever-popular Grand Marnier.

3	oranges	3	
1 cup	white granulated sugar	250 mL	
1	stick cinnamon	1	
1 tsp.	glycerin	5 mL	
2 cups	brandy	500 mL	

1. Carefully remove the peel from the oranges, taking care not to remove any of the white pith, as it will make the liqueur bitter. Juice oranges. Measure exactly 1 cup (250 mL) of orange juice.

2. Mix peel, juice, sugar and cinnamon together in a medium-sized bowl. Microwave on **HIGH** for 3 - 4 minutes or until the mixture comes to a rolling boil.

3. Boil for 30 seconds. Remove from the microwave and cool slightly. Add glycerin and brandy.

4. Pour into a jar or bottle and cap. Let stand for 1 month. After 1 month strain through fine cheesecloth. Pour back into bottle and serve as desired.

Makes 3½ cups. May be doubled.

RASPBERRY LIQUEUR

A pleasant-tasting liqueur which is delicious served over ice cream. Use in the Raspberry Chiffon Topping on page 23.

40 oz.	frozen raspberries	1.25 kg	
1½ cups	white granulated sugar	375 mL	
1 tsp.	glycerin	5 mL	
1½ cups	vodka	375 mL	

1. Mix undrained raspberries and sugar together in a medium-sized microwave-safe bowl. Microwave on **HIGH** for 7 - 8 minutes or until the mixture comes to a boil and boils for 2 minutes. Stir occasionally.

2. Remove from the microwave. Cool slightly. Add glycerin and vodka.

3. Pour into a jar or bottle and cap. Let stand for 2 weeks. Strain through a cheesecloth. Recap and let stand an additional 2 weeks before serving.

Makes 4 cups. May be doubled.

INDEX

123

125

Share LET'S MICROWAVE! with a friend

Please send me _____copies of LET'S MICROWAVE!, at $10.95 per book, plus $1.50 (total order) for postage and handling:

Number of books _____x $10.95 = _____

Postage and handling _____ = $ 1.50
Total enclosed _____ = _____
U.S. orders payable in U.S. funds — $8.95 U.S.   _____

NAME: _____

STREET: _____

CITY: _____ PROV./STATE _____

COUNTRY: _____ POSTAL CODE/ZIP: _____

Please make checks or money order payable to:
DELTA PUBLISHING LTD.
P.O. Box 5411, Station "A"
Calgary, Alberta, Canada   T2H 1X8

Price is subject to change
10% of the proceeds from all mail orders will be donated to the Canadian Progress Club, Calgary Eves, in support of the Aunts At Large Program.

....

Share LET'S MICROWAVE! with a friend

Please send me _____copies of LET'S MICROWAVE!, at $10.95 per book, plus $1.50 (total order) for postage and handling:

Number of books _____x $10.95 = _____

Postage and handling _____ = $ 1.50
Total enclosed _____ = _____
U.S. orders payable in U.S. funds — $8.95 U.S.   _____

NAME: _____

STREET: _____

CITY: _____ PROV./STATE _____

COUNTRY: _____ POSTAL CODE/ZIP: _____

Please make checks or money order payable to:
DELTA PUBLISHING LTD.
P.O. Box 5411, Station "A"
Calgary, Alberta, Canada   T2H 1X8

Price is subject to change
10% of the proceeds from all mail orders will be donated to the Canadian Progress Club, Calgary Eves, in support of the Aunts At Large Program.